AMERICAN
GOVERNMENT
The Basics

Jim Haight

Kendall Hunt
publishing company

Kendall Hunt
publishing company

www.kendallhunt.com
Send all inquiries to:
4050 Westmark Drive
Dubuque, IA 52004-1840

ISBN 978-1-4652-7516-5

Printed in the United States of America

Contents

Preface

Wouldn't you like a textbook that contains basic information, so an instructor can customize it his or her own way—one that is inexpensive and interactive, so students can take notes inside the text, and one that students will keep at the end of the course? This textbook is designed that way. It contains basic information so an instructor can add to the text any way he or she wants. It is interactive in that it provides pages for students to take notes throughout each chapter. It is cost effective and finally it is one that, I hope, students will want to keep once the course is over.

I must thank my parents, who are no longer with me, for instilling my values and teaching me what a work ethic is really about. For my wife, who is my inspiration every day, I say thank you for the wonderful life we have. Finally, I want to thank my daughter, son-in-law, and grand-children for keeping me grounded and teaching me what life is really about.

I hope that this textbook meets your expectations and helps you realize that getting involved in your government is all about your future and the future of your family. Why wouldn't you want to be a part of that?

The Constitution

THE CONSTITUTION OF THE UNITED STATES

WE THE PEOPLE of the United States, in Order to form a more perfect Union, establish Justice, insure domestic Tranquility, provide for the common defence, promote the general Welfare, and secure the Blessings of Liberty to ourselves and our Posterity, do ordain and establish this Constitution for the United States of America.

ARTICLE I

Section 1

All legislative Powers herein granted shall be vested in a Congress of the United States, which shall consist of a Senate and House of Representatives.

Section 2

The House of Representatives shall be composed of Members chosen every second Year by the People of the several States, and the Electors in each State shall have the Qualifications requisite for Electors of the most numerous Branch of the State Legislature.

No Person shall be a Representative who shall not have attained to the Age of twenty five Years, and been seven Years a Citizen of the United States, and who shall not, when elected, be an Inhabitant of that State in which he shall be chosen.

Representatives and direct Taxes shall be apportioned among the several States which may be included within this Union, according to their respective Numbers, which shall be determined by adding to the whole Number of free Persons, including those bound to Service for a Term of Years, and excluding Indians not taxed, three fifths of all other Persons. The actual Enumeration shall be made within three Years after the first Meeting of the Congress of the United States, and within every subsequent Term of ten Years, in such Manner as they shall by Law direct. The Number of Representatives shall not exceed one for every thirty Thousand, but each State shall have at Least one Representative; and until such enumeration shall be made, the State of New Hampshire shall be entitled to chuse three, Massachusetts eight, Rhode-Island and Providence Plantations one, Connecticut five, New-York six, New Jersey four, Pennsylvania eight, Delaware one, Maryland six, Virginia ten, North Carolina five, South Carolina five, and Georgia three.

When vacancies happen in the Representation from any State, the Executive Authority thereof shall issue Writs of Election to fill such Vacancies.

The House of Representatives shall chuse their Speaker and other Officers; and shall have the sole Power of Impeachment.

Section 3

The Senate of the United States shall be composed of two Senators from each State, chosen by the Legislature thereof, for six Years; and each Senator shall have one Vote.

Immediately after they shall be assembled in Consequence of the first Election, they shall be divided as equally as may be into three Classes. The Seats of the Senators of the first Class shall be

CLASS NOTES

vacated at the Expiration of the second Year, of the second Class at the Expiration of the fourth Year, and of the third Class at the Expiration of the sixth Year, so that one third may be chosen every second Year; and if Vacancies happen by Resignation, or otherwise, during the Recess of the Legislature of any State, the Executive thereof may make temporary Appointments until the next Meeting of the Legislature, which shall then fill such Vacancies.

No Person shall be a Senator who shall not have attained to the Age of thirty Years, and been nine Years a Citizen of the United States, and who shall not, when elected, be an Inhabitant of that State for which he shall be chosen.

The Vice President of the United States shall be President of the Senate, but shall have no Vote, unless they be equally divided.

The Senate shall chuse their other Officers, and also a President pro tempore, in the Absence of the Vice President, or when he shall exercise the Office of President of the United States.

The Senate shall have the sole Power to try all Impeachments. When sitting for that Purpose, they shall be on Oath or Affirmation. When the President of the United States is tried, the Chief Justice shall preside: And no Person shall be convicted without the Concurrence of two thirds of the Members present.

Judgment in Cases of Impeachment shall not extend further than to removal from Office, and disqualification to hold and enjoy any Office of honor, Trust or Profit under the United States: but the Party convicted shall nevertheless be liable and subject to Indictment, Trial, Judgment and Punishment, according to Law.

Section 4

The Times, Places and Manner of holding Elections for Senators and Representatives, shall be prescribed in each State by the Legislature thereof; but the Congress may at any time by Law make or alter such Regulations, except as to the Places of chusing Senators.

The Congress shall assemble at least once in every Year, and such Meeting shall be on the first Monday in December, unless they shall by Law appoint a different Day.

Section 5

Each House shall be the Judge of the Elections, Returns and Qualifications of its own Members, and a Majority of each shall constitute a Quorum to do Business; but a smaller Number may adjourn from day to day, and may be authorized to compel the Attendance of absent Members, in such Manner, and under such Penalties as each House may provide.

Each House may determine the Rules of its Proceedings, punish its Members for disorderly Behaviour, and, with the Concurrence of two thirds, expel a Member.

Each House shall keep a Journal of its Proceedings, and from time to time publish the same, excepting such Parts as may in their Judgment require Secrecy; and the Yeas and Nays of the Members of either House on any question shall, at the Desire of one fifth of those Present, be entered on the Journal.

Neither House, during the Session of Congress, shall, without the Consent of the other, adjourn for more than three days, nor to any other Place than that in which the two Houses shall be sitting.

CLASS NOTES

Section 6

The Senators and Representatives shall receive a Compensation for their Services, to be ascertained by Law, and paid out of the Treasury of the United States. They shall in all Cases, except Treason, Felony and Breach of the Peace, be privileged from Arrest during their Attendance at the Session of their respective Houses, and in going to and returning from the same; and for any Speech or Debate in either House, they shall not be questioned in any other Place.

No Senator or Representative shall, during the Time for which he was elected, be appointed to any civil Office under the Authority of the United States, which shall have been created, or the Emoluments whereof shall have been encreased during such time; and no Person holding any Office under the United States, shall be a Member of either House during his Continuance in Office.

Section 7

All Bills for raising Revenue shall originate in the House of Representatives; but the Senate may propose or concur with Amendments as on other Bills.

Every Bill which shall have passed the House of Representatives and the Senate, shall, before it become a Law, be presented to the President of the United States; If he approve he shall sign it, but if not he shall return it, with his Objections to that House in which it shall have originated, who shall enter the Objections at large on their Journal, and proceed to reconsider it. If after such Reconsideration two thirds of that House shall agree to pass the Bill, it shall be sent, together with the Objections, to the other House, by which it shall likewise be reconsidered, and if approved by two thirds of that House, it shall become a Law. But in all such Cases the Votes of both Houses shall be determined by yeas and Nays, and the Names of the Persons voting for and against the Bill shall be entered on the Journal of each House respectively. If any Bill shall not be returned by the President within ten Days (Sundays excepted) after it shall have been presented to him, the Same shall be a Law, in like Manner as if he had signed it, unless the Congress by their Adjournment prevent its Return, in which Case it shall not be a Law.

Every Order, Resolution, or Vote to which the Concurrence of the Senate and House of Representatives may be necessary (except on a question of Adjournment) shall be presented to the President of the United States; and before the Same shall take Effect, shall be approved by him, or being disapproved by him, shall be repassed by two thirds of the Senate and House of Representatives, according to the Rules and Limitations prescribed in the Case of a Bill.

Section 8

The Congress shall have Power To lay and collect Taxes, Duties, Imposts and Excises, to pay the Debts and provide for the common Defence and general Welfare of the United States; but all Duties, Imposts and Excises shall be uniform throughout the United States;

To borrow Money on the credit of the United States;

To regulate Commerce with foreign Nations, and among the several States, and with the Indian Tribes;

To establish an uniform Rule of Naturalization, and uniform Laws on the subject of Bankruptcies throughout the United States;

CLASS NOTES

To coin Money, regulate the Value thereof, and of foreign Coin, and fix the Standard of Weights and Measures;

To provide for the Punishment of counterfeiting the Securities and current Coin of the United States;

To establish Post Offices and post Roads;

To promote the Progress of Science and useful Arts, by securing for limited Times to Authors and Inventors the exclusive Right to their respective Writings and Discoveries;

To constitute Tribunals inferior to the supreme Court;

To define and punish Piracies and Felonies committed on the high Seas, and Offences against the Law of Nations;

To declare War, grant Letters of Marque and Reprisal, and make Rules concerning Captures on Land and Water;

To raise and support Armies, but no Appropriation of Money to that Use shall be for a longer Term than two Years;

To provide and maintain a Navy;

To make Rules for the Government and Regulation of the land and naval Forces;

To provide for calling forth the Militia to execute the Laws of the Union, suppress Insurrections and repel Invasions;

To provide for organizing, arming, and disciplining, the Militia, and for governing such Part of them as may be employed in the Service of the United States, reserving to the States respectively, the Appointment of the Officers, and the Authority of training the Militia according to the discipline prescribed by Congress;

To exercise exclusive Legislation in all Cases whatsoever, over such District (not exceeding ten Miles square) as may, by Cession of particular States, and the Acceptance of Congress, become the Seat of the Government of the United States, and to exercise like Authority over all Places purchased by the Consent of the Legislature of the State in which the Same shall be, for the Erection of Forts, Magazines, Arsenals, dock-Yards, and other needful Buildings;—And

To make all Laws which shall be necessary and proper for carrying into Execution the foregoing Powers, and all other Powers vested by this Constitution in the Government of the United States, or in any Department or Officer thereof.

Section 9

The Migration or Importation of such Persons as any of the States now existing shall think proper to admit, shall not be prohibited by the Congress prior to the Year one thousand eight hundred and eight, but a Tax or duty may be imposed on such Importation, not exceeding ten dollars for each Person.

The Privilege of the Writ of Habeas Corpus shall not be suspended, unless when in Cases of Rebellion or Invasion the public Safety may require it.

No Bill of Attainder or ex post facto Law shall be passed.

No Capitation, or other direct, Tax shall be laid, unless in Proportion to the Census or enumeration herein before directed to be taken.

No Tax or Duty shall be laid on Articles exported from any State.

CLASS NOTES

No Preference shall be given by any Regulation of Commerce or Revenue to the Ports of one State over those of another: nor shall Vessels bound to, or from, one State, be obliged to enter, clear, or pay Duties in another.

No Money shall be drawn from the Treasury, but in Consequence of Appropriations made by Law; and a regular Statement and Account of the Receipts and Expenditures of all public Money shall be published from time to time.

No Title of Nobility shall be granted by the United States: And no Person holding any Office of Profit or Trust under them, shall, without the Consent of the Congress, accept of any present, Emolument, Office, or Title, of any kind whatever, from any King, Prince, or foreign State.

Section 10

No State shall enter into any Treaty, Alliance, or Confederation; grant Letters of Marque and Reprisal; coin Money; emit Bills of Credit; make any Thing but gold and silver Coin a Tender in Payment of Debts; pass any Bill of Attainder, ex post facto Law, or Law impairing the Obligation of Contracts, or grant any Title of Nobility.

No State shall, without the Consent of the Congress, lay any Imposts or Duties on Imports or Exports, except what may be absolutely necessary for executing it's inspection Laws: and the net Produce of all Duties and Imposts, laid by any State on Imports or Exports, shall be for the Use of the Treasury of the United States; and all such Laws shall be subject to the Revision and Controul of the Congress.

No State shall, without the Consent of Congress, lay any Duty of Tonnage, keep Troops, or Ships of War in time of Peace, enter into any Agreement or Compact with another State, or with a foreign Power, or engage in War, unless actually invaded, or in such imminent Danger as will not admit of delay.

ARTICLE II

Section 1

The executive Power shall be vested in a President of the United States of America. He shall hold his Office during the Term of four Years, and, together with the Vice President, chosen for the same Term, be elected, as follows

Each State shall appoint, in such Manner as the Legislature thereof may direct, a Number of Electors, equal to the whole Number of Senators and Representatives to which the State may be entitled in the Congress: but no Senator or Representative, or Person holding an Office of Trust or Profit under the United States, shall be appointed an Elector.

The Electors shall meet in their respective States, and vote by Ballot for two Persons, of whom one at least shall not be an Inhabitant of the same State with themselves. And they shall make a List of all the Persons voted for, and of the Number of Votes for each; which List they shall sign and certify, and transmit sealed to the Seat of the Government of the United States, directed to the President of the Senate. The President of the Senate shall, in the Presence of the Senate and House of Representatives, open all the Certificates, and the Votes shall then be counted. The Person having the greatest Number of Votes shall be the President, if such Number be a Majority of

CLASS NOTES

_____

_____

_____

_____

_____

_____

_____

_____

_____

_____

_____

_____

_____

_____

_____

_____

_____

_____

_____

the whole Number of Electors appointed; and if there be more than one who have such Majority, and have an equal Number of Votes, then the House of Representatives shall immediately chuse by Ballot one of them for President; and if no Person have a Majority, then from the five highest on the List the said House shall in like Manner chuse the President. But in chusing the President, the Votes shall be taken by States, the Representation from each State having one Vote; A quorum for this Purpose shall consist of a Member or Members from two thirds of the States, and a Majority of all the States shall be necessary to a Choice. In every Case, after the Choice of the President, the Person having the greatest Number of Votes of the Electors shall be the Vice President. But if there should remain two or more who have equal Votes, the Senate shall chuse from them by Ballot the Vice President.

The Congress may determine the Time of chusing the Electors, and the Day on which they shall give their Votes; which Day shall be the same throughout the United States.

No Person except a natural born Citizen, or a Citizen of the United States, at the time of the Adoption of this Constitution, shall be eligible to the Office of President; neither shall any Person be eligible to that Office who shall not have attained to the Age of thirty five Years, and been fourteen Years a Resident within the United States.

In Case of the Removal of the President from Office, or of his Death, Resignation, or Inability to discharge the Powers and Duties of the said Office, the Same shall devolve on the Vice President, and the Congress may by Law provide for the Case of Removal, Death, Resignation or Inability, both of the President and Vice President, declaring what Officer shall then act as President, and such Officer shall act accordingly, until the Disability be removed, or a President shall be elected.

The President shall, at stated Times, receive for his Services, a Compensation, which shall neither be encreased nor diminished during the Period for which he shall have been elected, and he shall not receive within that Period any other Emolument from the United States, or any of them.

Before he enter on the Execution of his Office, he shall take the following Oath or Affirmation:—"I do solemnly swear (or affirm) that I will faithfully execute the Office of President of the United States, and will to the best of my Ability, preserve, protect and defend the Constitution of the United States."

Section 2

The President shall be Commander in Chief of the Army and Navy of the United States, and of the Militia of the several States, when called into the actual Service of the United States; he may require the Opinion, in writing, of the principal Officer in each of the executive Departments, upon any Subject relating to the Duties of their respective Offices, and he shall have Power to grant Reprieves and Pardons for Offences against the United States, except in Cases of Impeachment.

He shall have Power, by and with the Advice and Consent of the Senate, to make Treaties, provided two thirds of the Senators present concur; and he shall nominate, and by and with the Advice and Consent of the Senate, shall appoint Ambassadors, other public Ministers and Consuls, Judges of the supreme Court, and all other Officers of the United States, whose Appointments are not herein otherwise provided for, and which shall be established by Law: but the

CLASS NOTES

Congress may by Law vest the Appointment of such inferior Officers, as they think proper, in the President alone, in the Courts of Law, or in the Heads of Departments.

The President shall have Power to fill up all Vacancies that may happen during the Recess of the Senate, by granting Commissions which shall expire at the End of their next Session.

Section 3

He shall from time to time give to the Congress Information of the State of the Union, and recommend to their Consideration such Measures as he shall judge necessary and expedient; he may, on extraordinary Occasions, convene both Houses, or either of them, and in Case of Disagreement between them, with Respect to the Time of Adjournment, he may adjourn them to such Time as he shall think proper; he shall receive Ambassadors and other public Ministers; he shall take Care that the Laws be faithfully executed, and shall Commission all the Officers of the United States.

Section 4

The President, Vice President and all civil Officers of the United States, shall be removed from Office on Impeachment for, and Conviction of, Treason, Bribery, or other high Crimes and Misdemeanors.

ARTICLE III

Section 1

The judicial Power of the United States, shall be vested in one supreme Court, and in such inferior Courts as the Congress may from time to time ordain and establish. The Judges, both of the supreme and inferior Courts, shall hold their Offices during good Behaviour, and shall, at stated Times, receive for their Services, a Compensation, which shall not be diminished during their Continuance in Office.

Section 2

The judicial Power shall extend to all Cases, in Law and Equity, arising under this Constitution, the Laws of the United States, and Treaties made, or which shall be made, under their Authority;—to all Cases affecting Ambassadors, other public Ministers and Consuls;—to all Cases of admiralty and maritime Jurisdiction;—to Controversies to which the United States shall be a Party;—to Controversies between two or more States;—between a State and Citizens of another State,—between Citizens of different States,—between Citizens of the same State claiming Lands under Grants of different States, and between a State, or the Citizens thereof, and foreign States, Citizens or Subjects.

In all Cases affecting Ambassadors, other public Ministers and Consuls, and those in which a State shall be Party, the supreme Court shall have original Jurisdiction. In all the other Cases before mentioned, the supreme Court shall have appellate Jurisdiction, both as to Law and Fact, with such Exceptions, and under such Regulations as the Congress shall make.

CLASS NOTES

The Trial of all Crimes, except in Cases of Impeachment, shall be by Jury; and such Trial shall be held in the State where the said Crimes shall have been committed; but when not committed within any State, the Trial shall be at such Place or Places as the Congress may by Law have directed.

Section 3

Treason against the United States, shall consist only in levying War against them, or in adhering to their Enemies, giving them Aid and Comfort. No Person shall be convicted of Treason unless on the Testimony of two Witnesses to the same overt Act, or on Confession in open Court.

The Congress shall have Power to declare the Punishment of Treason, but no Attainder of Treason shall work Corruption of Blood, or Forfeiture except during the Life of the Person attainted.

ARTICLE IV

Section 1

Full Faith and Credit shall be given in each State to the public Acts, Records, and judicial Proceedings of every other State. And the Congress may by general Laws prescribe the Manner in which such Acts, Records and Proceedings shall be proved, and the Effect thereof.

Section 2

The Citizens of each State shall be entitled to all Privileges and Immunities of Citizens in the several States.

A Person charged in any State with Treason, Felony, or other Crime, who shall flee from Justice, and be found in another State, shall on Demand of the executive Authority of the State from which he fled, be delivered up, to be removed to the State having Jurisdiction of the Crime.

No Person held to Service or Labour in one State, under the Laws thereof, escaping into another, shall, in Consequence of any Law or Regulation therein, be discharged from such Service or Labour, but shall be delivered up on Claim of the Party to whom such Service or Labour may be due.

Section 3

New States may be admitted by the Congress into this Union; but no new State shall be formed or erected within the Jurisdiction of any other State; nor any State be formed by the Junction of two or more States, or Parts of States, without the Consent of the Legislatures of the States concerned as well as of the Congress.

The Congress shall have Power to dispose of and make all needful Rules and Regulations respecting the Territory or other Property belonging to the United States; and nothing in this Constitution shall be so construed as to Prejudice any Claims of the United States, or of any particular State.

CLASS NOTES

Section 4

The United States shall guarantee to every State in this Union a Republican Form of Government, and shall protect each of them against Invasion; and on Application of the Legislature, or of the Executive (when the Legislature cannot be convened), against domestic Violence.

ARTICLE V

The Congress, whenever two thirds of both Houses shall deem it necessary, shall propose Amendments to this Constitution, or, on the Application of the Legislatures of two thirds of the several States, shall call a Convention for proposing Amendments, which, in either Case, shall be valid to all Intents and Purposes, as Part of this Constitution, when ratified by the Legislatures of three fourths of the several States, or by Conventions in three fourths thereof, as the one or the other Mode of Ratification may be proposed by the Congress; Provided that no Amendment which may be made prior to the Year One thousand eight hundred and eight shall in any Manner affect the first and fourth Clauses in the Ninth Section of the first Article; and that no State, without its Consent, shall be deprived of its equal Suffrage in the Senate.

ARTICLE VI

All Debts contracted and Engagements entered into, before the Adoption of this Constitution, shall be as valid against the United States under this Constitution, as under the Confederation.

This Constitution, and the Laws of the United States which shall be made in Pursuance thereof; and all Treaties made, or which shall be made, under the Authority of the United States, shall be the supreme Law of the Land; and the Judges in every State shall be bound thereby, any Thing in the Constitution or Laws of any State to the Contrary notwithstanding.

The Senators and Representatives before mentioned, and the Members of the several State Legislatures, and all executive and judicial Officers, both of the United States and of the several States, shall be bound by Oath or Affirmation, to support this Constitution; but no religious Test shall ever be required as a Qualification to any Office or public Trust under the United States.

ARTICLE VII

The Ratification of the Conventions of nine States, shall be sufficient for the Establishment of this Constitution between the States so ratifying the Same.

The Word, "the," being interlined between the seventh and eighth Lines of the first Page, The Word "Thirty" being partly written on an Erazure in the fifteenth Line of the first Page, The Words "is tried" being interlined between the thirty second and thirty third Lines of the first Page and the Word "the" being interlined between the forty third and forty fourth Lines of the second Page.

CLASS NOTES

Attest William Jackson Secretary

Done in Convention by the Unanimous Consent of the States present the Seventeenth Day of September in the Year of our Lord one thousand seven hundred and Eighty seven and of the Independance of the United States of America the Twelfth In witness whereof We have hereunto subscribed our Names,

G. Washington
Presidt and deputy from Virginia

Delaware
Geo: Read
Gunning Bedford jun
John Dickinson
Richard Bassett
Jaco: Broom

Maryland
James McHenry
Dan of St Thos. Jenifer
Danl. Carroll

Virginia
John Blair
James Madison Jr.

North Carolina
Wm. Blount
Richd. Dobbs Spaight
Hu Williamson

South Carolina
J. Rutledge
Charles Cotesworth Pinckney
Charles Pinckney
Pierce Butler

Georgia
William Few
Abr Baldwin

New Hampshire
John Langdon
Nicholas Gilman

Massachusetts
Nathaniel Gorham
Rufus King

Connecticut
Wm. Saml. Johnson
Roger Sherman

New York
Alexander Hamilton

New Jersey
Wil: Livingston
David Brearley
Wm. Paterson
Jona: Dayton

Pensylvania
B Franklin
Thomas Mifflin
Robt. Morris
Geo. Clymer
Thos. FitzSimons
Jared Ingersoll
James Wilson
Gouv Morris

CLASS NOTES

_____

_____

_____

_____

_____

_____

_____

_____

_____

_____

_____

_____

_____

_____

_____

_____

_____

_____

_____

_____

_____

_____

INTRODUCTION   The **Constitution** of the United States of America was **ratified** in 1787. It combined ideas from many people and from documents including the Articles of Confederation and the Declaration of Independence. The **Founding Fathers** and the **Framers** are the individuals credited with the ideas and the writing of the Constitution. The Constitution is one of the greatest examples of **compromise** that this nation has ever seen. The original document did not set forth any requirements for voting and the term democracy does not appear anywhere in the document. The question to ask yourself is "should the Constitution adapt to the times, the times to the Constitution, or can it be both?"

PREAMBLE

The **Preamble** is the statement at the beginning of the Constitution that states the source of its authority and the purpose it is to serve. It gives the source of its authority as the people of the United States. It lists as its goals to "establish Justice, insure domestic Tranquility, provide for the common defense, promote the general Welfare, and secure the Blessings of Liberty." These goals are designed to "form a more perfect union" and they are for the people of the United States and their future generations.

BASIC PRINCIPLES OF THE CONSTITUTION

The basic principles of the Constitution are **popular sovereignty, federalism, limited government, separation of powers, checks and balances,** and **judicial review.** The following chart illustrates separation of powers and checks and balances.

Executive Branch (Enforces Laws)	Executive Checks Legislative	Executive Checks Judicial
Shutterstock/Orhan Cam	• Can veto laws • Can recommend legislation • Carries out laws • Can call Congress into special session • Makes appointments to federal posts • Negotiates treaties	• Appoints federal judges • Carries out court decisions

(Continued)

CLASS NOTES

Legislative Branch (Makes Laws)	Legislative Checks Executive	Legislative Checks Judicial
Shutterstock/Erika Cross	• Can override presidential veto • Confirms appointments • Ratifies treaties • Appropriates money • Can impeach and remove the President • Can investigate executive actions	• Approves judicial appointments • Creates lower federal courts • Can impeach and remove judges • May rewrite legislation interpreted by the courts
Judicial Branch (Interprets Laws)	Judicial Checks Executive	Judicial Checks Legislative
Shutterstock/Joe Ravi	• May declare actions of executive agencies unconstitutional • May declare presidential actions unconstitutional	• Can declare acts of Congress unconstitutional

ARTICLES OF THE CONSTITUTION

The Constitution is composed of seven articles. Each article discusses an important aspect of the Constitution. The articles are

Article I (the Legislative Branch)   discusses details of the House of Representatives and Senate including the bicameral legislature, requirements and terms of office, methods of selection and apportionment, enumerated powers, implied powers, and **Necessary and Proper Clause**.

Article II (the Executive Branch)   discusses details for the presidency including the requirements and term of office, the **Electoral College**, the powers and duties of the President, and the **State of the Union Address**.

Article III (the Judicial Branch)   discusses the details for establishing the Judicial Branch including the Supreme Court, its jurisdiction, and the role of Congress.

Article IV (relations of the states to each other)   discusses the **Full Faith and Credit Clause**.

Article V (amending the Constitution)   discusses how the Constitution can be changed. This is a two-step process where an amendment is proposed and then ratified. The proposal can be by a 2/3 vote in both houses of Congress or by 2/3 of the state legislatures that request a special convention. An amendment is ratified by a 3/4 vote of the state legislatures or a 3/4 vote of special state conventions.

Article VI (Supremacy Clause)   discusses how the Constitution is the supreme law of the land.

Article VII (ratifying the Constitution)   discusses how the Constitution is to be ratified.

CLASS NOTES

THE BILL OF RIGHTS (1–10)

The **Bill of Rights** consists of the first 10 amendments to the Constitution. The following chart lists the amendments and the rights given by that amendment.

1st Amendment	Freedom of religion, speech, and the press; rights of assembly and petition
2nd Amendment	Right to bear arms
3rd Amendment	Housing of soldiers
4th Amendment	Search and arrest warrants
5th Amendment	Rights in criminal cases
6th Amendment	Rights to a fair trial
7th Amendment	Rights in civil cases
8th Amendment	Bails, fines, and punishments
9th Amendment	Rights retained by the people
10th Amendment	Powers retained by the states and the people

REMAINING AMENDMENTS (11–27)

The remaining amendments protect civil rights as well as relate to the selection of government officials or the operation of the branches of government. There are also amendments that address specific public policies. The following chart lists these remaining amendments.

11th Amendment	Lawsuits against states
12th Amendment	Election of the President and Vice President
13th Amendment	Abolition of slavery
14th Amendment	Civil rights
15th Amendment	**Suffrage** (race, color, or previous condition of servitude)
16th Amendment	Income taxes
17th Amendment	Direct election of senators
18th Amendment	Prohibition of liquor
19th Amendment	Suffrage (women)
20th Amendment	Terms of the President and Congress
21st Amendment	Repeal of prohibition (18th Amendment)

(Continued)

CLASS NOTES

22nd Amendment	Limitation of presidential terms
23rd Amendment	Suffrage (District of Columbia)
24th Amendment	**Poll taxes**
25th Amendment	Presidential disability and succession
26th Amendment	Suffrage (18-year-olds)
27th Amendment	Congressional salaries

CHALLENGES TO THE CONSTITUTION

- Interpretation by the courts
- Social and cultural change
- Changes in technology

THE DECLARATION OF INDEPENDENCE: A TRANSCRIPTION

IN CONGRESS, July 4, 1776.

The unanimous Declaration of the thirteen united States of America,

When in the Course of human events, it becomes necessary for one people to dissolve the political bands which have connected them with another, and to assume among the powers of the earth, the separate and equal station to which the Laws of Nature and of Nature's God entitle them, a decent respect to the opinions of mankind requires that they should declare the causes which impel them to the separation.

We hold these truths to be self-evident, that all men are created equal, that they are endowed by their Creator with certain unalienable Rights, that among these are Life, Liberty and the pursuit of Happiness.—That to secure these rights, Governments are instituted among Men, deriving their just powers from the consent of the governed,—That whenever any Form of Government becomes destructive of these ends, it is the Right of the People to alter or to abolish it, and to institute new Government, laying its foundation on such principles and organizing its powers in such form, as to them shall seem most likely to effect their Safety and Happiness. Prudence, indeed, will dictate that Governments long established should not be changed for light and transient causes; and accordingly all experience hath shewn, that mankind are more disposed to suffer, while evils are sufferable, than to right themselves by abolishing the forms to which they are accustomed. But when a long train of abuses and usurpations, pursuing invariably the same Object evinces a design to reduce them under absolute Despotism, it is their right, it is their duty, to throw off such Government, and to provide new Guards for their future security.—Such has been the patient sufferance of these Colonies; and such is now the necessity which constrains them to alter their former Systems of Government. The history of the present King of Great Britain is a history of repeated injuries and usurpations, all having in direct object

CLASS NOTES

the establishment of an absolute Tyranny over these States. To prove this, let Facts be submitted to a candid world.

He has refused his Assent to Laws, the most wholesome and necessary for the public good.

He has forbidden his Governors to pass Laws of immediate and pressing importance, unless suspended in their operation till his Assent should be obtained; and when so suspended, he has utterly neglected to attend to them.

He has refused to pass other Laws for the accommodation of large districts of people, unless those people would relinquish the right of Representation in the Legislature, a right inestimable to them and formidable to tyrants only.

He has called together legislative bodies at places unusual, uncomfortable, and distant from the depository of their public Records, for the sole purpose of fatiguing them into compliance with his measures.

He has dissolved Representative Houses repeatedly, for opposing with manly firmness his invasions on the rights of the people.

He has refused for a long time, after such dissolutions, to cause others to be elected; whereby the Legislative powers, incapable of Annihilation, have returned to the People at large for their exercise; the State remaining in the mean time exposed to all the dangers of invasion from without, and convulsions within.

He has endeavoured to prevent the population of these States; for that purpose obstructing the Laws for Naturalization of Foreigners; refusing to pass others to encourage their migrations hither, and raising the conditions of new Appropriations of Lands.

He has obstructed the Administration of Justice, by refusing his Assent to Laws for establishing Judiciary powers.

He has made Judges dependent on his Will alone, for the tenure of their offices, and the amount and payment of their salaries.

He has erected a multitude of New Offices, and sent hither swarms of Officers to harrass our people, and eat out their substance.

He has kept among us, in times of peace, Standing Armies without the Consent of our legislatures.

He has affected to render the Military independent of and superior to the Civil power.

He has combined with others to subject us to a jurisdiction foreign to our constitution, and unacknowledged by our laws; giving his Assent to their Acts of pretended Legislation:

For Quartering large bodies of armed troops among us:

For protecting them, by a mock Trial, from punishment for any Murders which they should commit on the Inhabitants of these States:

For cutting off our Trade with all parts of the world:

For imposing Taxes on us without our Consent:

For depriving us in many cases, of the benefits of Trial by Jury:

For transporting us beyond Seas to be tried for pretended offences

For abolishing the free System of English Laws in a neighbouring Province, establishing therein an Arbitrary government, and enlarging its Boundaries so as to render it at once an example and fit instrument for introducing the same absolute rule into these Colonies:

CLASS NOTES

For taking away our Charters, abolishing our most valuable Laws, and altering fundamentally the Forms of our Governments:

For suspending our own Legislatures, and declaring themselves invested with power to legislate for us in all cases whatsoever.

He has abdicated Government here, by declaring us out of his Protection and waging War against us.

He has plundered our seas, ravaged our Coasts, burnt our towns, and destroyed the lives of our people.

He is at this time transporting large Armies of foreign Mercenaries to compleat the works of death, desolation and tyranny, already begun with circumstances of Cruelty & perfidy scarcely paralleled in the most barbarous ages, and totally unworthy the Head of a civilized nation.

He has constrained our fellow Citizens taken Captive on the high Seas to bear Arms against their Country, to become the executioners of their friends and Brethren, or to fall themselves by their Hands.

He has excited domestic insurrections amongst us, and has endeavoured to bring on the inhabitants of our frontiers, the merciless Indian Savages, whose known rule of warfare, is an undistinguished destruction of all ages, sexes and conditions.

In every stage of these Oppressions We have Petitioned for Redress in the most humble terms: Our repeated Petitions have been answered only by repeated injury. A Prince whose character is thus marked by every act which may define a Tyrant, is unfit to be the ruler of a free people.

Nor have We been wanting in attentions to our Brittish brethren. We have warned them from time to time of attempts by their legislature to extend an unwarrantable jurisdiction over us. We have reminded them of the circumstances of our emigration and settlement here. We have appealed to their native justice and magnanimity, and we have conjured them by the ties of our common kindred to disavow these usurpations, which, would inevitably interrupt our connections and correspondence. They too have been deaf to the voice of justice and of consanguinity. We must, therefore, acquiesce in the necessity, which denounces our Separation, and hold them, as we hold the rest of mankind, Enemies in War, in Peace Friends.

We, therefore, the Representatives of the united States of America, in General Congress, Assembled, appealing to the Supreme Judge of the world for the rectitude of our intentions, do, in the Name, and by Authority of the good People of these Colonies, solemnly publish and declare, That these United Colonies are, and of Right ought to be Free and Independent States; that they are Absolved from all Allegiance to the British Crown, and that all political connection between them and the State of Great Britain, is and ought to be totally dissolved; and that as Free and Independent States, they have full Power to levy War, conclude Peace, contract Alliances, establish Commerce, and to do all other Acts and Things which Independent States may of right do. And for the support of this Declaration, with a firm reliance on the protection of divine Providence, we mutually pledge to each other our Lives, our Fortunes and our sacred Honor.

CLASS NOTES

The 56 signatures on the Declaration appear in the positions indicated:

Column 1
Georgia:
  Button Gwinnett
  Lyman Hall
  George Walton

Column 2
North Carolina:
  William Hooper
  Joseph Hewes
  John Penn
South Carolina:
  Edward Rutledge
  Thomas Heyward, Jr.
  Thomas Lynch, Jr.
  Arthur Middleton

Column 3
Massachusetts:
  John Hancock
Maryland:
  Samuel Chase
  William Paca
  Thomas Stone
  Charles Carroll of Carrollton
Virginia:
  George Wythe
  Richard Henry Lee
  Thomas Jefferson
  Benjamin Harrison
  Thomas Nelson, Jr.
  Francis Lightfoot Lee
  Carter Braxton

Column 4
Pennsylvania:
  Robert Morris
  Benjamin Rush
  Benjamin Franklin
  John Morton
  George Clymer

James Smith
George Taylor
James Wilson
George Ross
Delaware:
  Caesar Rodney
  George Read
  Thomas McKean

Column 5
New York:
  William Floyd
  Philip Livingston
  Francis Lewis
  Lewis Morris
New Jersey:
  Richard Stockton
  John Witherspoon
  Francis Hopkinson
  John Hart
  Abraham Clark

Column 6
New Hampshire:
  Josiah Bartlett
  William Whipple
Massachusetts:
  Samuel Adams
  John Adams
  Robert Treat Paine
  Elbridge Gerry
Rhode Island:
  Stephen Hopkins
  William Ellery
Connecticut:
  Roger Sherman
  Samuel Huntington
  William Williams
  Oliver Wolcott
New Hampshire:
  Matthew Thornton

CLASS NOTES

FEDERALIST PAPER #10

The Same Subject Continued: The Union as a Safeguard Against Domestic Faction and Insurrection
From the New York Packet.
Friday, November 23, 1787.
Author: **James Madison**

To the People of the State of New York:

AMONG the numerous advantages promised by a well-constructed Union, none deserves to be more accurately developed than its tendency to break and control the violence of faction. The friend of popular governments never finds himself so much alarmed for their character and fate, as when he contemplates their propensity to this dangerous vice. He will not fail, therefore, to set a due value on any plan which, without violating the principles to which he is attached, provides a proper cure for it. The instability, injustice, and confusion introduced into the public councils, have, in truth, been the mortal diseases under which popular governments have everywhere perished; as they continue to be the favorite and fruitful topics from which the adversaries to liberty derive their most specious declamations. The valuable improvements made by the American constitutions on the popular models, both ancient and modern, cannot certainly be too much admired; but it would be an unwarrantable partiality, to contend that they have as effectually obviated the danger on this side, as was wished and expected. Complaints are everywhere heard from our most considerate and virtuous citizens, equally the friends of public and private faith, and of public and personal liberty, that our governments are too unstable, that the public good is disregarded in the conflicts of rival parties, and that measures are too often decided, not according to the rules of justice and the rights of the minor party, but by the superior force of an interested and overbearing majority. However anxiously we may wish that these complaints had no foundation, the evidence, of known facts will not permit us to deny that they are in some degree true. It will be found, indeed, on a candid review of our situation, that some of the distresses under which we labor have been erroneously charged on the operation of our governments; but it will be found, at the same time, that other causes will not alone account for many of our heaviest misfortunes; and, particularly, for that prevailing and increasing distrust of public engagements, and alarm for private rights, which are echoed from one end of the continent to the other. These must be chiefly, if not wholly, effects of the unsteadiness and injustice with which a factious spirit has tainted our public administrations.

By a faction, I understand a number of citizens, whether amounting to a majority or a minority of the whole, who are united and actuated by some common impulse of passion, or of interest, adversed to the rights of other citizens, or to the permanent and aggregate interests of the community.

There are two methods of curing the mischiefs of faction: the one, by removing its causes; the other, by controlling its effects.

There are again two methods of removing the causes of faction: the one, by destroying the liberty which is essential to its existence; the other, by giving to every citizen the same opinions, the same passions, and the same interests.

CLASS NOTES

It could never be more truly said than of the first remedy, that it was worse than the disease. Liberty is to faction what air is to fire, an aliment without which it instantly expires. But it could not be less folly to abolish liberty, which is essential to political life, because it nourishes faction, than it would be to wish the annihilation of air, which is essential to animal life, because it imparts to fire its destructive agency.

The second expedient is as impracticable as the first would be unwise. As long as the reason of man continues fallible, and he is at liberty to exercise it, different opinions will be formed. As long as the connection subsists between his reason and his self-love, his opinions and his passions will have a reciprocal influence on each other; and the former will be objects to which the latter will attach themselves. The diversity in the faculties of men, from which the rights of property originate, is not less an insuperable obstacle to a uniformity of interests. The protection of these faculties is the first object of government. From the protection of different and unequal faculties of acquiring property, the possession of different degrees and kinds of property immediately results; and from the influence of these on the sentiments and views of the respective proprietors, ensues a division of the society into different interests and parties.

The latent causes of faction are thus sown in the nature of man; and we see them everywhere brought into different degrees of activity, according to the different circumstances of civil society. A zeal for different opinions concerning religion, concerning government, and many other points, as well of speculation as of practice; an attachment to different leaders ambitiously contending for pre-eminence and power; or to persons of other descriptions whose fortunes have been interesting to the human passions, have, in turn, divided mankind into parties, inflamed them with mutual animosity, and rendered them much more disposed to vex and oppress each other than to co-operate for their common good. So strong is this propensity of mankind to fall into mutual animosities, that where no substantial occasion presents itself, the most frivolous and fanciful distinctions have been sufficient to kindle their unfriendly passions and excite their most violent conflicts. But the most common and durable source of factions has been the various and unequal distribution of property. Those who hold and those who are without property have ever formed distinct interests in society. Those who are creditors, and those who are debtors, fall under a like discrimination. A landed interest, a manufacturing interest, a mercantile interest, a moneyed interest, with many lesser interests, grow up of necessity in civilized nations, and divide them into different classes, actuated by different sentiments and views. The regulation of these various and interfering interests forms the principal task of modern legislation, and involves the spirit of party and faction in the necessary and ordinary operations of the government.

No man is allowed to be a judge in his own cause, because his interest would certainly bias his judgment, and, not improbably, corrupt his integrity. With equal, nay with greater reason, a body of men are unfit to be both judges and parties at the same time; yet what are many of the most important acts of legislation, but so many judicial determinations, not indeed concerning the rights of single persons, but concerning the rights of large bodies of citizens? And what are the different classes of legislators but advocates and parties to the causes which they determine? Is a law proposed concerning private debts? It is a question to which the creditors are parties on one side and the debtors on the other. Justice ought to hold the balance between them. Yet the parties are, and must be, themselves the judges; and the most numerous party, or, in other words, the most powerful faction must be expected to prevail. Shall domestic manufactures be

CLASS NOTES

encouraged, and in what degree, by restrictions on foreign manufactures? are questions which would be differently decided by the landed and the manufacturing classes, and probably by neither with a sole regard to justice and the public good. The apportionment of taxes on the various descriptions of property is an act which seems to require the most exact impartiality; yet there is, perhaps, no legislative act in which greater opportunity and temptation are given to a predominant party to trample on the rules of justice. Every shilling with which they overburden the inferior number, is a shilling saved to their own pockets.

It is in vain to say that enlightened statesmen will be able to adjust these clashing interests, and render them all subservient to the public good. Enlightened statesmen will not always be at the helm. Nor, in many cases, can such an adjustment be made at all without taking into view indirect and remote considerations, which will rarely prevail over the immediate interest which one party may find in disregarding the rights of another or the good of the whole.

The inference to which we are brought is, that the CAUSES of faction cannot be removed, and that relief is only to be sought in the means of controlling its EFFECTS.

If a faction consists of less than a majority, relief is supplied by the republican principle, which enables the majority to defeat its sinister views by regular vote. It may clog the administration, it may convulse the society; but it will be unable to execute and mask its violence under the forms of the Constitution. When a majority is included in a faction, the form of popular government, on the other hand, enables it to sacrifice to its ruling passion or interest both the public good and the rights of other citizens. To secure the public good and private rights against the danger of such a faction, and at the same time to preserve the spirit and the form of popular government, is then the great object to which our inquiries are directed. Let me add that it is the great desideratum by which this form of government can be rescued from the opprobrium under which it has so long labored, and be recommended to the esteem and adoption of mankind.

By what means is this object attainable? Evidently by one of two only. Either the existence of the same passion or interest in a majority at the same time must be prevented, or the majority, having such coexistent passion or interest, must be rendered, by their number and local situation, unable to concert and carry into effect schemes of oppression. If the impulse and the opportunity be suffered to coincide, we well know that neither moral nor religious motives can be relied on as an adequate control. They are not found to be such on the injustice and violence of individuals, and lose their efficacy in proportion to the number combined together, that is, in proportion as their efficacy becomes needful.

From this view of the subject it may be concluded that a pure democracy, by which I mean a society consisting of a small number of citizens, who assemble and administer the government in person, can admit of no cure for the mischiefs of faction. A common passion or interest will, in almost every case, be felt by a majority of the whole; a communication and concert result from the form of government itself; and there is nothing to check the inducements to sacrifice the weaker party or an obnoxious individual. Hence it is that such democracies have ever been spectacles of turbulence and contention; have ever been found incompatible with personal security or the rights of property; and have in general been as short in their lives as they have been violent in their deaths. Theoretic politicians, who have patronized this species of government, have erroneously supposed that by reducing mankind to a perfect equality in their political rights, they would, at the same time, be perfectly equalized and assimilated in their possessions, their opinions, and their passions.

CLASS NOTES

A republic, by which I mean a government in which the scheme of representation takes place, opens a different prospect, and promises the cure for which we are seeking. Let us examine the points in which it varies from pure democracy, and we shall comprehend both the nature of the cure and the efficacy which it must derive from the Union.

The two great points of difference between a democracy and a republic are: first, the delegation of the government, in the latter, to a small number of citizens elected by the rest; secondly, the greater number of citizens, and greater sphere of country, over which the latter may be extended.

The effect of the first difference is, on the one hand, to refine and enlarge the public views, by passing them through the medium of a chosen body of citizens, whose wisdom may best discern the true interest of their country, and whose patriotism and love of justice will be least likely to sacrifice it to temporary or partial considerations. Under such a regulation, it may well happen that the public voice, pronounced by the representatives of the people, will be more consonant to the public good than if pronounced by the people themselves, convened for the purpose. On the other hand, the effect may be inverted. Men of factious tempers, of local prejudices, or of sinister designs, may, by intrigue, by corruption, or by other means, first obtain the suffrages, and then betray the interests, of the people. The question resulting is, whether small or extensive republics are more favorable to the election of proper guardians of the public weal; and it is clearly decided in favor of the latter by two obvious considerations:

In the first place, it is to be remarked that, however small the republic may be, the representatives must be raised to a certain number, in order to guard against the cabals of a few; and that, however large it may be, they must be limited to a certain number, in order to guard against the confusion of a multitude. Hence, the number of representatives in the two cases not being in proportion to that of the two constituents, and being proportionally greater in the small republic, it follows that, if the proportion of fit characters be not less in the large than in the small republic, the former will present a greater option, and consequently a greater probability of a fit choice.

In the next place, as each representative will be chosen by a greater number of citizens in the large than in the small republic, it will be more difficult for unworthy candidates to practice with success the vicious arts by which elections are too often carried; and the suffrages of the people being more free, will be more likely to centre in men who possess the most attractive merit and the most diffusive and established characters.

It must be confessed that in this, as in most other cases, there is a mean, on both sides of which inconveniences will be found to lie. By enlarging too much the number of electors, you render the representatives too little acquainted with all their local circumstances and lesser interests; as by reducing it too much, you render him unduly attached to these, and too little fit to comprehend and pursue great and national objects. The federal Constitution forms a happy combination in this respect; the great and aggregate interests being referred to the national, the local and particular to the State legislatures.

The other point of difference is, the greater number of citizens and extent of territory which may be brought within the compass of republican than of democratic government; and it is this circumstance principally which renders factious combinations less to be dreaded in the former than in the latter. The smaller the society, the fewer probably will be the distinct parties and interests composing it; the fewer the distinct parties and interests, the more frequently will a majority be found of the same party; and the smaller the number of individuals composing a majority,

CLASS NOTES

and the smaller the compass within which they are placed, the more easily will they concert and execute their plans of oppression. Extend the sphere, and you take in a greater variety of parties and interests; you make it less probable that a majority of the whole will have a common motive to invade the rights of other citizens; or if such a common motive exists, it will be more difficult for all who feel it to discover their own strength, and to act in unison with each other. Besides other impediments, it may be remarked that, where there is a consciousness of unjust or dishonorable purposes, communication is always checked by distrust in proportion to the number whose concurrence is necessary.

Hence, it clearly appears, that the same advantage which a republic has over a democracy, in controlling the effects of faction, is enjoyed by a large over a small republic,—is enjoyed by the Union over the States composing it. Does the advantage consist in the substitution of representatives whose enlightened views and virtuous sentiments render them superior to local prejudices and schemes of injustice? It will not be denied that the representation of the Union will be most likely to possess these requisite endowments. Does it consist in the greater security afforded by a greater variety of parties, against the event of any one party being able to outnumber and oppress the rest? In an equal degree does the increased variety of parties comprised within the Union, increase this security. Does it, in fine, consist in the greater obstacles opposed to the concert and accomplishment of the secret wishes of an unjust and interested majority? Here, again, the extent of the Union gives it the most palpable advantage.

The influence of factious leaders may kindle a flame within their particular States, but will be unable to spread a general conflagration through the other States. A religious sect may degenerate into a political faction in a part of the Confederacy; but the variety of sects dispersed over the entire face of it must secure the national councils against any danger from that source. A rage for paper money, for an abolition of debts, for an equal division of property, or for any other improper or wicked project, will be less apt to pervade the whole body of the Union than a particular member of it; in the same proportion as such a malady is more likely to taint a particular county or district, than an entire State.

In the extent and proper structure of the Union, therefore, we behold a republican remedy for the diseases most incident to republican government. And according to the degree of pleasure and pride we feel in being republicans, ought to be our zeal in cherishing the spirit and supporting the character of Federalists.

FEDERALIST PAPER #51

The Structure of the Government Must Furnish the Proper Checks and Balances Between the Different Departments
From the New York Packet.
Friday, February 8, 1788.
Author: **Alexander Hamilton** or **James Madison**

To the People of the State of New York:
TO WHAT expedient, then, shall we finally resort, for maintaining in practice the necessary partition of power among the several departments, as laid down in the Constitution? The only answer that can be given is, that as all these exterior provisions are found to be inadequate, the

CLASS NOTES

defect must be supplied, by so contriving the interior structure of the government as that its several constituent parts may, by their mutual relations, be the means of keeping each other in their proper places. Without presuming to undertake a full development of this important idea, I will hazard a few general observations, which may perhaps place it in a clearer light, and enable us to form a more correct judgment of the principles and structure of the government planned by the convention. In order to lay a due foundation for that separate and distinct exercise of the different powers of government, which to a certain extent is admitted on all hands to be essential to the preservation of liberty, it is evident that each department should have a will of its own; and consequently should be so constituted that the members of each should have as little agency as possible in the appointment of the members of the others. Were this principle rigorously adhered to, it would require that all the appointments for the supreme executive, legislative, and judiciary magistracies should be drawn from the same fountain of authority, the people, through channels having no communication whatever with one another. Perhaps such a plan of constructing the several departments would be less difficult in practice than it may in contemplation appear. Some difficulties, however, and some additional expense would attend the execution of it. Some deviations, therefore, from the principle must be admitted. In the constitution of the judiciary department in particular, it might be inexpedient to insist rigorously on the principle: first, because peculiar qualifications being essential in the members, the primary consideration ought to be to select that mode of choice which best secures these qualifications; secondly, because the permanent tenure by which the appointments are held in that department, must soon destroy all sense of dependence on the authority conferring them. It is equally evident, that the members of each department should be as little dependent as possible on those of the others, for the emoluments annexed to their offices. Were the executive magistrate, or the judges, not independent of the legislature in this particular, their independence in every other would be merely nominal. But the great security against a gradual concentration of the several powers in the same department, consists in giving to those who administer each department the necessary constitutional means and personal motives to resist encroachments of the others. The provision for defense must in this, as in all other cases, be made commensurate to the danger of attack. Ambition must be made to counteract ambition. The interest of the man must be connected with the constitutional rights of the place. It may be a reflection on human nature, that such devices should be necessary to control the abuses of government. But what is government itself, but the greatest of all reflections on human nature? If men were angels, no government would be necessary. If angels were to govern men, neither external nor internal controls on government would be necessary. In framing a government which is to be administered by men over men, the great difficulty lies in this: you must first enable the government to control the governed; and in the next place oblige it to control itself. A dependence on the people is, no doubt, the primary control on the government; but experience has taught mankind the necessity of auxiliary precautions. This policy of supplying, by opposite and rival interests, the defect of better motives, might be traced through the whole system of human affairs, private as well as public. We see it particularly displayed in all the subordinate distributions of power, where the constant aim is to divide and arrange the several offices in such a manner as that each may be a check on the other that the private interest of every individual may be a sentinel over the public rights. These inventions of prudence cannot be less requisite in the distribution of the supreme powers of the State. But it is not possible to give to each department an equal power of self-defense. In republican

CLASS NOTES

_____

_____

_____

_____

_____

_____

_____

_____

_____

_____

_____

_____

_____

_____

_____

_____

_____

_____

government, the legislative authority necessarily predominates. The remedy for this inconveniency is to divide the legislature into different branches; and to render them, by different modes of election and different principles of action, as little connected with each other as the nature of their common functions and their common dependence on the society will admit. It may even be necessary to guard against dangerous encroachments by still further precautions. As the weight of the legislative authority requires that it should be thus divided, the weakness of the executive may require, on the other hand, that it should be fortified. An absolute negative on the legislature appears, at first view, to be the natural defense with which the executive magistrate should be armed. But perhaps it would be neither altogether safe nor alone sufficient. On ordinary occasions it might not be exerted with the requisite firmness, and on extraordinary occasions it might be perfidiously abused. May not this defect of an absolute negative be supplied by some qualified connection between this weaker department and the weaker branch of the stronger department, by which the latter may be led to support the constitutional rights of the former, without being too much detached from the rights of its own department? If the principles on which these observations are founded be just, as I persuade myself they are, and they be applied as a criterion to the several State constitutions, and to the federal Constitution it will be found that if the latter does not perfectly correspond with them, the former are infinitely less able to bear such a test. There are, moreover, two considerations particularly applicable to the federal system of America, which place that system in a very interesting point of view. First. In a single republic, all the power surrendered by the people is submitted to the administration of a single government; and the usurpations are guarded against by a division of the government into distinct and separate departments. In the compound republic of America, the power surrendered by the people is first divided between two distinct governments, and then the portion allotted to each subdivided among distinct and separate departments. Hence a double security arises to the rights of the people. The different governments will control each other, at the same time that each will be controlled by itself. Second. It is of great importance in a republic not only to guard the society against the oppression of its rulers, but to guard one part of the society against the injustice of the other part. Different interests necessarily exist in different classes of citizens. If a majority be united by a common interest, the rights of the minority will be insecure. There are but two methods of providing against this evil: the one by creating a will in the community independent of the majority that is, of the society itself; the other, by comprehending in the society so many separate descriptions of citizens as will render an unjust combination of a majority of the whole very improbable, if not impracticable. The first method prevails in all governments possessing an hereditary or self-appointed authority. This, at best, is but a precarious security; because a power independent of the society may as well espouse the unjust views of the major, as the rightful interests of the minor party, and may possibly be turned against both parties. The second method will be exemplified in the federal republic of the United States. Whilst all authority in it will be derived from and dependent on the society, the society itself will be broken into so many parts, interests, and classes of citizens, that the rights of individuals, or of the minority, will be in little danger from interested combinations of the majority. In a free government the security for civil rights must be the same as that for religious rights. It consists in the one case in the multiplicity of interests, and in the other in the multiplicity of sects. The degree of security in both cases will depend on the number of interests and sects; and this may be presumed to depend on the extent of country and number of people comprehended under the same government. This

CLASS NOTES

_____

_____

_____

_____

_____

_____

_____

_____

_____

_____

_____

_____

_____

_____

_____

_____

_____

_____

view of the subject must particularly recommend a proper federal system to all the sincere and considerate friends of republican government, since it shows that in exact proportion as the territory of the Union may be formed into more circumscribed Confederacies, or States oppressive combinations of a majority will be facilitated: the best security, under the republican forms, for the rights of every class of citizens, will be diminished: and consequently the stability and independence of some member of the government, the only other security, must be proportionately increased. Justice is the end of government. It is the end of civil society. It ever has been and ever will be pursued until it be obtained, or until liberty be lost in the pursuit. In a society under the forms of which the stronger faction can readily unite and oppress the weaker, anarchy may as truly be said to reign as in a state of nature, where the weaker individual is not secured against the violence of the stronger; and as, in the latter state, even the stronger individuals are prompted, by the uncertainty of their condition, to submit to a government which may protect the weak as well as themselves; so, in the former state, will the more powerful factions or parties be gradnally induced, by a like motive, to wish for a government which will protect all parties, the weaker as well as the more powerful. It can be little doubted that if the State of Rhode Island was separated from the Confederacy and left to itself, the insecurity of rights under the popular form of government within such narrow limits would be displayed by such reiterated oppressions of factious majorities that some power altogether independent of the people would soon be called for by the voice of the very factions whose misrule had proved the necessity of it. In the extended republic of the United States, and among the great variety of interests, parties, and sects which it embraces, a coalition of a majority of the whole society could seldom take place on any other principles than those of justice and the general good; whilst there being thus less danger to a minor from the will of a major party, there must be less pretext, also, to provide for the security of the former, by introducing into the government a will not dependent on the latter, or, in other words, a will independent of the society itself. It is no less certain than it is important, notwithstanding the contrary opinions which have been entertained, that the larger the society, provided it lie within a practical sphere, the more duly capable it will be of self-government. And happily for the REPUBLICAN CAUSE, the practicable sphere may be carried to a very great extent, by a judicious modification and mixture of the FEDERAL PRINCIPLE.
PUBLIUS.

FEDERALIST PAPER #78

The Judiciary Department
From McLEAN'S Edition, New York.
Author: **Alexander Hamilton**

To the People of the State of New York:

WE PROCEED now to an examination of the judiciary department of the proposed government.

In unfolding the defects of the existing Confederation, the utility and necessity of a federal judicature have been clearly pointed out. It is the less necessary to recapitulate the considerations there urged, as the propriety of the institution in the abstract is not disputed; the only questions

CLASS NOTES

which have been raised being relative to the manner of constituting it, and to its extent. To these points, therefore, our observations shall be confined.

The manner of constituting it seems to embrace these several objects: 1st. The mode of appointing the judges. 2d. The tenure by which they are to hold their places. 3d. The partition of the judiciary authority between different courts, and their relations to each other.

First. As to the mode of appointing the judges; this is the same with that of appointing the officers of the Union in general, and has been so fully discussed in the two last numbers, that nothing can be said here which would not be useless repetition.

Second. As to the tenure by which the judges are to hold their places; this chiefly concerns their duration in office; the provisions for their support; the precautions for their responsibility.

According to the plan of the convention, all judges who may be appointed by the United States are to hold their offices DURING GOOD BEHAVIOR; which is conformable to the most approved of the State constitutions and among the rest, to that of this State. Its propriety having been drawn into question by the adversaries of that plan, is no light symptom of the rage for objection, which disorders their imaginations and judgments. The standard of good behavior for the continuance in office of the judicial magistracy, is certainly one of the most valuable of the modern improvements in the practice of government. In a monarchy it is an excellent barrier to the despotism of the prince; in a republic it is a no less excellent barrier to the encroachments and oppressions of the representative body. And it is the best expedient which can be devised in any government, to secure a steady, upright, and impartial administration of the laws.

Whoever attentively considers the different departments of power must perceive, that, in a government in which they are separated from each other, the judiciary, from the nature of its functions, will always be the least dangerous to the political rights of the Constitution; because it will be least in a capacity to annoy or injure them. The Executive not only dispenses the honors, but holds the sword of the community. The legislature not only commands the purse, but pre-scribes the rules by which the duties and rights of every citizen are to be regulated. The judiciary, on the contrary, has no influence over either the sword or the purse; no direction either of the strength or of the wealth of the society; and can take no active resolution whatever. It may truly be said to have neither FORCE nor WILL, but merely judgment; and must ultimately depend upon the aid of the executive arm even for the efficacy of its judgments.

This simple view of the matter suggests several important consequences. It proves incontest-ably, that the judiciary is beyond comparison the weakest of the three departments of power; that it can never attack with success either of the other two; and that all possible care is requisite to enable it to defend itself against their attacks. It equally proves, that though individual oppres-sion may now and then proceed from the courts of justice, the general liberty of the people can never be endangered from that quarter; I mean so long as the judiciary remains truly distinct from both the legislature and the Executive. For I agree, that "there is no liberty, if the power of judging be not separated from the legislative and executive powers." And it proves, in the last place, that as liberty can have nothing to fear from the judiciary alone, but would have every thing to fear from its union with either of the other departments; that as all the effects of such a union must ensue from a dependence of the former on the latter, notwithstanding a nominal and apparent separation; that as, from the natural feebleness of the judiciary, it is in continual jeop-ardy of being overpowered, awed, or influenced by its co-ordinate branches; and that as nothing can contribute so much to its firmness and independence as permanency in office, this quality

CLASS NOTES

may therefore be justly regarded as an indispensable ingredient in its constitution, and, in a great measure, as the citadel of the public justice and the public security.

The complete independence of the courts of justice is peculiarly essential in a limited Constitution. By a limited Constitution, I understand one which contains certain specified exceptions to the legislative authority; such, for instance, as that it shall pass no bills of attainder, no ex-post-facto laws, and the like. Limitations of this kind can be preserved in practice no other way than through the medium of courts of justice, whose duty it must be to declare all acts contrary to the manifest tenor of the Constitution void. Without this, all the reservations of particular rights or privileges would amount to nothing.

Some perplexity respecting the rights of the courts to pronounce legislative acts void, because contrary to the Constitution, has arisen from an imagination that the doctrine would imply a superiority of the judiciary to the legislative power. It is urged that the authority which can declare the acts of another void, must necessarily be superior to the one whose acts may be declared void. As this doctrine is of great importance in all the American constitutions, a brief discussion of the ground on which it rests cannot be unacceptable.

There is no position which depends on clearer principles, than that every act of a delegated authority, contrary to the tenor of the commission under which it is exercised, is void. No legislative act, therefore, contrary to the Constitution, can be valid. To deny this, would be to affirm, that the deputy is greater than his principal; that the servant is above his master; that the representatives of the people are superior to the people themselves; that men acting by virtue of powers, may do not only what their powers do not authorize, but what they forbid.

If it be said that the legislative body are themselves the constitutional judges of their own powers, and that the construction they put upon them is conclusive upon the other departments, it may be answered, that this cannot be the natural presumption, where it is not to be collected from any particular provisions in the Constitution. It is not otherwise to be supposed, that the Constitution could intend to enable the representatives of the people to substitute their WILL to that of their constituents. It is far more rational to suppose, that the courts were designed to be an intermediate body between the people and the legislature, in order, among other things, to keep the latter within the limits assigned to their authority. The interpretation of the laws is the proper and peculiar province of the courts. A constitution is, in fact, and must be regarded by the judges, as a fundamental law. It therefore belongs to them to ascertain its meaning, as well as the meaning of any particular act proceeding from the legislative body. If there should happen to be an irreconcilable variance between the two, that which has the superior obligation and validity ought, of course, to be preferred; or, in other words, the Constitution ought to be preferred to the statute, the intention of the people to the intention of their agents.

Nor does this conclusion by any means suppose a superiority of the judicial to the legislative power. It only supposes that the power of the people is superior to both; and that where the will of the legislature, declared in its statutes, stands in opposition to that of the people, declared in the Constitution, the judges ought to be governed by the latter rather than the former. They ought to regulate their decisions by the fundamental laws, rather than by those which are not fundamental.

This exercise of judicial discretion, in determining between two contradictory laws, is exemplified in a familiar instance. It not uncommonly happens, that there are two statutes existing at one time, clashing in whole or in part with each other, and neither of them containing any

CLASS NOTES

repealing clause or expression. In such a case, it is the province of the courts to liquidate and fix their meaning and operation. So far as they can, by any fair construction, be reconciled to each other, reason and law conspire to dictate that this should be done; where this is impracticable, it becomes a matter of necessity to give effect to one, in exclusion of the other. The rule which has obtained in the courts for determining their relative validity is, that the last in order of time shall be preferred to the first. But this is a mere rule of construction, not derived from any positive law, but from the nature and reason of the thing. It is a rule not enjoined upon the courts by legislative provision, but adopted by themselves, as consonant to truth and propriety, for the direction of their conduct as interpreters of the law. They thought it reasonable, that between the interfering acts of an EQUAL authority, that which was the last indication of its will should have the preference.

But in regard to the interfering acts of a superior and subordinate authority, of an original and derivative power, the nature and reason of the thing indicate the converse of that rule as proper to be followed. They teach us that the prior act of a superior ought to be preferred to the subsequent act of an inferior and subordinate authority; and that accordingly, whenever a particular statute contravenes the Constitution, it will be the duty of the judicial tribunals to adhere to the latter and disregard the former.

It can be of no weight to say that the courts, on the pretense of a repugnancy, may substitute their own pleasure to the constitutional intentions of the legislature. This might as well happen in the case of two contradictory statutes; or it might as well happen in every adjudication upon any single statute. The courts must declare the sense of the law; and if they should be disposed to exercise WILL instead of JUDGMENT, the consequence would equally be the substitution of their pleasure to that of the legislative body. The observation, if it prove any thing, would prove that there ought to be no judges distinct from that body.

If, then, the courts of justice are to be considered as the bulwarks of a limited Constitution against legislative encroachments, this consideration will afford a strong argument for the permanent tenure of judicial offices, since nothing will contribute so much as this to that independent spirit in the judges which must be essential to the faithful performance of so arduous a duty.

This independence of the judges is equally requisite to guard the Constitution and the rights of individuals from the effects of those ill humors, which the arts of designing men, or the influence of particular conjunctures, sometimes disseminate among the people themselves, and which, though they speedily give place to better information, and more deliberate reflection, have a tendency, in the meantime, to occasion dangerous innovations in the government, and serious oppressions of the minor party in the community. Though I trust the friends of the proposed Constitution will never concur with its enemies, in questioning that fundamental principle of republican government, which admits the right of the people to alter or abolish the established Constitution, whenever they find it inconsistent with their happiness, yet it is not to be inferred from this principle, that the representatives of the people, whenever a momentary inclination happens to lay hold of a majority of their constituents, incompatible with the provisions in the existing Constitution, would, on that account, be justifiable in a violation of those provisions; or that the courts would be under a greater obligation to connive at infractions in this shape, than when they had proceeded wholly from the cabals of the representative body. Until the people have, by some solemn and authoritative act, annulled or changed the established form, it

CLASS NOTES

is binding upon themselves collectively, as well as individually; and no presumption, or even knowledge, of their sentiments, can warrant their representatives in a departure from it, prior to such an act. But it is easy to see, that it would require an uncommon portion of fortitude in the judges to do their duty as faithful guardians of the Constitution, where legislative invasions of it had been instigated by the major voice of the community.

But it is not with a view to infractions of the Constitution only, that the independence of the judges may be an essential safeguard against the effects of occasional ill humors in the society. These sometimes extend no farther than to the injury of the private rights of particular classes of citizens, by unjust and partial laws. Here also the firmness of the judicial magistracy is of vast importance in mitigating the severity and confining the operation of such laws. It not only serves to moderate the immediate mischiefs of those which may have been passed, but it operates as a check upon the legislative body in passing them; who, perceiving that obstacles to the success of iniquitous intention are to be expected from the scruples of the courts, are in a manner compelled, by the very motives of the injustice they meditate, to qualify their attempts. This is a circumstance calculated to have more influence upon the character of our governments, than but few may be aware of. The benefits of the integrity and moderation of the judiciary have already been felt in more States than one; and though they may have displeased those whose sinister expectations they may have disappointed, they must have commanded the esteem and applause of all the virtuous and disinterested. Considerate men, of every description, ought to prize whatever will tend to beget or fortify that temper in the courts: as no man can be sure that he may not be to-morrow the victim of a spirit of injustice, by which he may be a gainer to-day. And every man must now feel, that the inevitable tendency of such a spirit is to sap the foundations of public and private confidence, and to introduce in its stead universal distrust and distress.

That inflexible and uniform adherence to the rights of the Constitution, and of individuals, which we perceive to be indispensable in the courts of justice, can certainly not be expected from judges who hold their offices by a temporary commission. Periodical appointments, however regulated, or by whomsoever made, would, in some way or other, be fatal to their necessary independence. If the power of making them was committed either to the Executive or legislature, there would be danger of an improper complaisance to the branch which possessed it; if to both, there would be an unwillingness to hazard the displeasure of either; if to the people, or to persons chosen by them for the special purpose, there would be too great a disposition to consult popularity, to justify a reliance that nothing would be consulted but the Constitution and the laws.

There is yet a further and a weightier reason for the permanency of the judicial offices, which is deducible from the nature of the qualifications they require. It has been frequently remarked, with great propriety, that a voluminous code of laws is one of the inconveniences necessarily connected with the advantages of a free government. To avoid an arbitrary discretion in the courts, it is indispensable that they should be bound down by strict rules and precedents, which serve to define and point out their duty in every particular case that comes before them; and it will readily be conceived from the variety of controversies which grow out of the folly and wickedness of mankind, that the records of those precedents must unavoidably swell to a very considerable bulk, and must demand long and laborious study to acquire a competent knowledge of them. Hence it is, that there can be but few men in the society who will have sufficient skill in the laws

CLASS NOTES

to qualify them for the stations of judges. And making the proper deductions for the ordinary depravity of human nature, the number must be still smaller of those who unite the requisite integrity with the requisite knowledge. These considerations apprise us, that the government can have no great option between fit character; and that a temporary duration in office, which would naturally discourage such characters from quitting a lucrative line of practice to accept a seat on the bench, would have a tendency to throw the administration of justice into hands less able, and less well qualified, to conduct it with utility and dignity. In the present circumstances of this country, and in those in which it is likely to be for a long time to come, the disadvantages on this score would be greater than they may at first sight appear; but it must be confessed, that they are far inferior to those which present themselves under the other aspects of the subject.

Upon the whole, there can be no room to doubt that the convention acted wisely in copying from the models of those constitutions which have established GOOD BEHAVIOR as the tenure of their judicial offices, in point of duration; and that so far from being blamable on this account, their plan would have been inexcusably defective, if it had wanted this important feature of good government. The experience of Great Britain affords an illustrious comment on the excellence of the institution.

PUBLIUS.

CLASS NOTES

protection
regulate in
viduals declared hu

governr

horities disclose
perty lawyer def
hts legal private

INTRODUCTION   In the early history of the country, the belief was that the states had the right to disobey the national government if they felt it had exceeded its powers or they could use the doctrine of **nullification**. Since that time, we have seen **dual federalism**, **cooperative federalism**, and **competitive federalism** become the dominant doctrines.

POWERS FOR THE NATIONAL GOVERNMENT
(Enumerated Powers)

The chief powers given to the national government by the Constitution are

- collect taxes
- borrow money on the credit of the United States
- regulate foreign and interstate commerce
- establish rules of **naturalization**
- coin money and regulate its value
- establish a post office
- establish lower courts under the Supreme Court
- declare and conduct war
- provide for an army and navy
- make all laws necessary and proper to carry out the enumerated powers

POWERS FOR THE STATE GOVERNMENTS
(Reserved Powers)

The chief powers given to the state governments by the Constitution are

- set times, places, and manner of elections as well as appoint electors
- ratify amendments to the Constitution
- establish local governments
- regulate intrastate commerce
- public education
- provide for public health, safety, and morals
- regulate marriage
- professional licenses
- conduct all powers not granted to the national government or denied to the states

CLASS NOTES

POWERS FOR THE NATIONAL AND STATE GOVERNMENTS
(Concurrent Powers)

- collect taxes
- regulate banks
- establish courts
- make and enforce laws
- borrow money
- provide for the common good

DOES FEDERALISM WORK?

Federalism usually works because states recognize that the Constitution and all national laws are "the supreme law of the land." Competition between the national government and the states usually stays in check and federalism works. The reasons for this are

- state and local governments assist the national government
- national, state, and local governments all have distinct resources and services
- interest groups provide a voice for the state and local governments

Unfortunately, there are times that federalism does not work like it is supposed to. Hurricane Katrina is a perfect example of this as authorities did not know which level of government should be in charge of the rescue attempts. There are political differences that hinder the success of federalism. The Democrats like policies to be set by the national government. They like national standards that provide consistency for the state and local governments. The Republicans like less centralization and endorse **devolution.** They feel that the states can handle most things better than the national government.

CLASS NOTES

CHAPTER 3
Civil Liberties

INTRODUCTION Civil liberties are contained in the Bill of Rights. When the Bill of Rights was written, the framers did not face all the complex issues that we face today. These issues are still covered by the liberties contained in the Bill of Rights even though some of these liberties are not specifically listed. What are the boundaries of these liberties and when do they infringe on other liberties are the questions we must ask and try to answer.

1ST AMENDMENT GUARANTEES
Freedom of Religion, Speech, and the Press; Rights of Assembly and Petition

Religion

Establishment Clause   (the government cannot establish or sanction an official religion)

Free Exercise Clause   (the government will not interfere with the practice of religion)

- Not absolute guarantee
- Has it become freedom of religion or freedom from religion?

Speech, Press, Assembly, and Petition

Speech and Press

  Protected Speech and Press
  - Limited **prior restraint**
  - **Symbolic speech**
  - **Hate speech**

  Unprotected Speech and Press
  - **Libel** and **Slander**
  - **Fighting words**
  - Obscenity
    - *Miller v California* (1973)

Assembly and Petition
- People's right to protest v government's right to limit dissent in name of security
- Based on peaceful conduct

CLASS NOTES

pentagon paper official rand.

lead. to the congress about the war in Vietnam.

. 2012 said on senate floors, 6:50

2ND AMENDMENT GUARANTEES
Right to Bear Arms

Interpreted as written or unlimited right?

4TH AMENDMENT
Search and Arrest Warrants

No unreasonable search or seizure

- can search person arrested
- can search things in plain view
- can search places or things accused can reach

Warrantless search are legal in certain situations

- consent, probable cause, or reasonable suspicion

Drunk driving stops

- field sobriety test or blood test

Drug testing

- legal at work and schools

Exclusionary Rule

- anything seized illegally cannot be used in court
- *Mapp v Ohio* (1961)

5TH AMENDMENT GUARANTEES
Self-Incrimination, Double Jeopardy, Eminent Domain

Miranda Warning

- your right to remain silent and not incrimination yourself
- *Miranda v Arizona* (1966)

Double Jeopardy

- can't be tried twice for the same crime

Eminent Domain

- the right of the government to take private property for public use
- *Kelo v City of New London* (2005) defined eminent domain even more

CLASS NOTES

_____

_____

_____

_____

_____

_____

_____

_____

_____

_____

_____

_____

_____

_____

_____

_____

_____

_____

_____

6TH AMENDMENT GUARANTEES
Fair Trial and Counsel

- right to a jury trial with a impartial jury of peers
- defendants have a right to an attorney and will be provided one if needed
  - *Gideon v Wainwright* (1963)

8TH AMENDMENT GUARANTEES
No Excessive Bail/No Cruel or Unusual Punishment

Death Penalty Methods (not all are used)

- Hanging
- Firing squad
- Gas chamber
- Electric chair
- Lethal injection

Is the death penalty effective as a deterrent?

RIGHT TO PRIVACY
Not Specifically Stated in the Bill of Rights

Abortion

- *Roe v Wade* (1973)

  right to privacy case and not pro-life v pro-choice

CIVIL LIBERTIES AND TERRORISM

USA Patriot Act

Does it violate the 1st and 4th Amendments as well as **due process**?

CLASS NOTES

CHAPTER 4

Civil Rights

RSITY

OPPORTUNITIES

DIFFERENT

EQUALITY

IRNESS

HORITY

FREEDOM

LAW

HUMAN

PARTNERSHIP

INTRODUCTION   Civil rights are the rights of individuals against discriminatory treatment based on race, sex, national origin, age, religion, or sexual orientation. The civil rights movement has been equated with the African-American push for equality after the Civil War. The 14th Amendment's equal protection clause guarantees introduced the idea of equality into the Constitution. We have seen more civil rights movements and more groups seek and have been granted these protections.

THE AFRICAN-AMERICAN MOVEMENT

The African-American movement really started with the three Civil War Amendments. They are

- 13th—outlawed slavery and "involuntary servitude"
- 14th—contains three key clauses
  - anyone born in the United States is a citizen and anyone residing in a state is a citizen of that state
  - bars states from depriving anyone, whether a citizen or not, of "life, liberty, or property, without due process of law"
  - holds that a state may not "deny to any person within its jurisdiction the equal protection of the laws
- 15th—the government cannot infringe on a citizen's right to vote "on account of race, color, or previous condition of servitude"

Although these amendments advanced equality for the former slaves, there were still many barriers for them to overcome. The *Plessy v Ferguson* case upheld the doctrine of "separate but equal" thereby making it legal to separate the races. This ruling was overturned by the *Brown v Board of Education of Topeka Kansas* case. There were many advances as many African-Americans moved northward during WWI and found fewer restrictions on their freedoms and Thurgood Marshall became the first African-American Supreme Court justice. Even with these advances the **Jim Crow** system was still in effect, especially in the south. After WWII, the push for equality created mass protests and boycotts. Rosa Parks became a rallying cry for the movement when she refused to give up her seat on a bus to a white man and was arrested. The NAACP, the National Association for the Advancement of Colored People, sued the city of Montgomery, Alabama and started a boycott led by Martin Luther King Jr. When the Supreme Court declared Montgomery's segregated public transportation system unconstitutional the boycott ended. It lasted 381 days. Martin Luther King Jr. was 26 years old and fresh out of divinity school when he became involved in the Montgomery boycott. He founded the Southern Christian Leadership Conference (SCLC) and he called for nonviolent protests. Martin Luther King Jr. and the SCLC conducted sit-ins

CLASS NOTES

and boycotts of businesses in Birmingham, Alabama and these protests and the violent police response pushed President Kennedy to propose civil rights legislation. The Civil Right Act was passed in 1964 and did the following:

- outlawed discrimination in voter registration
- banned discrimination on the basis of "race, color, religion, or national origin" in public accommodations and employment
- authorized the Justice Department to initiate lawsuits to desegregate public facilities and schools
- provided for the withholding of federal funds from discriminatory state and local programs
- set up the Equal Employment Opportunity Commission (EEOC) to implement the law

The Voting Rights Act of 1965 outlawed literacy tests and required states to prove to the Justice Department that any changes in their voting practices would not abridge anyone's right to vote. Affirmative Actions has been the main focus recently as well as equality in the justice system.

THE WOMEN'S MOVEMENT

This movement began during the push to do away with slavery and women had hoped to obtain the right to vote, but they were not included in the 15th Amendment. Women did not get the right to vote until the 19th Amendment was passed in 1920. An Equal Rights Amendment was proposed in 1923 and it mandated the equal treatment of men and women. It was finally passed by Congress in 1972 and sent to the states for ratification but was defeated in 1982. Title VII of the Civil Rights Act of 1964 prohibits gender discrimination by private employers. The Equal Pay Act of 1963 requires employers to pay men and women the same pay for equal work. The Lilly Ledbetter Fair Pay Act allows for the filing of unfair pay complaints within 180 days of each discriminatory paycheck. Title IX bars educational institutions receiving federal funding from discriminating against female students.

HISPANIC-AMERICANS

Hispanics are the largest and fastest growing minority group in the United States and politicians see them as growing group of voters. Immigration laws and reform have become the biggest controversy for the Hispanic community. States are passing immigration laws as they feel the federal government is not enforcing the federal laws and the federal government is suing the states on the basis that immigration is a federal issue and not a state issue.

AMERICANS WITH DISABILITIES

People with disabilities have pushed for anti-discrimination laws to give them equal protection. The Americans with Disabilities Act (ADA) defines a disabled person as one with a physical or mental impairment that limits one or more "life activities," or who has a record of such

CLASS NOTES

impairments. It guarantees access to public facilities and employment as well as requires employers to make the necessary changes to their equipment or schedules for people with disabilities. The biggest controversy is "what is a disability?"

GAYS AND LESBIANS

The gay and lesbian community has faced discrimination in employment, insurance survivor benefits, and now marriage. The "Don't Ask, Don't Tell" policy was implemented by President Clinton in order to ban discrimination against gays and lesbians in the military. In 2010, this policy was declared unconstitutional by a federal judge and was done away with by President Obama. Many states are now approving of same-sex marriages and the courts are ruling that laws banning these marriages are unconstitutional. Until now, the Supreme Court has not ruled on this, but may in the future.

Other groups have faced battles with discrimination such as the American Indian and Asian-Americans. **Affirmation action** policies have been used to give special treatment to all of the groups that have been discriminated against. Many of these policies have been challenged such as the Texas Law School affirmative action admission program and by the following court cases:

Regents of the University of California v Bakke

Grutter v Bollinger

CLASS NOTES

Media and Its Influence

INTRODUCTION   News, as reported by the media, is a selective account by journalists of what happens. Since most people get their news about the government and politics through the media, it has become vital to the political process to understand the role and goal of the media because the two are interrelated. **Mass media** was the norm for bringing the news to people. Technology introduced **new media** into the equation. **Social media**, for some, has become the new norm. The questions to ask yourself is "Can you watch conservative news if you are liberal and liberal news if you are conservative?" If you can't then you will only follow the views of those that believe the same as you. By doing so, you never challenge your own views. By challenging your own views, you either question them or reinforce them. Which is better?

ROLE OF THE MEDIA

The role of the media is to inform the public, but its goal is to be profitable. Without reaching this goal, they can never fulfill their role. In order to reach their goal, the media must rely on advertisers as the main source of money. Many times this can discourage the media from reporting on and being critical of challenging political and social issues since their advertisers might have different views and pull their funding. Competition to attract viewers has led to **narrowcasting** as well as the increase in the use of experts and citizens as journalists.

TYPES OF MEDIA

There are many different types of media. They are

- mass media (print media, radio, and television)
- new media (internet, blogs, and social networking)

JOURNALISTS AND REPORTING

Journalists are limited in how they report by government regulations and the "Code of Ethics" published by the Society of Professional Journalists. They are also limited by space and time constraints. **Objectivity** becomes an issue as journalists race to report a story first. In reporting ethically, journalists must obtain information **"on the record"** or **"off the record."** Many times they get their political information from a **press release, press briefing,** or **press conference** and use **sound bites** for effect. Journalists not only report the news but also rely on **talking-heads, pundits, partisans,** and **experts.** These people give their opinions while commenting on the news and many times put their own **spin** on the news. The media has become a **watchdog** and **attack dog** in dealing with political issues.

CLASS NOTES

(handwritten note) _tattoo gun_

CHAPTER 6

Political Culture and Socialization in a Changing Population

INTRODUCTION   As the population of the United States increases and becomes more of a **melting pot**, our **political culture** is constantly changing and being challenged. The views people have about the government and how it operates comes from their personal experiences and upbringing. These are the views we discuss and pass on to others, but where exactly do the experiences come from and how does our upbringing impact them?

POLITICAL CULTURE

Since political culture is the ideologies, beliefs, customs, and traditions of a nation, they change in response to events such as war, changes in the economy, as well as changes in technology. Government decisions based on these events influence how people view their government. Many people have developed national pride and the term **American exceptionalism** has been used in both positive and negative ways. Symbols and heroes help to create national pride. Our political culture is based on many things such as

- geographic region
- demographic characteristics
- personal and social characteristics
- religion

Many times conflicts arise as these groups compete for the resources in society.

POLITICAL SOCIALIZATION

Political socialization is the process by which people learn about their government. It is also the way people get their beliefs, attitudes, values, and behaviors that we associate with being a good citizen. This process also stresses the values of a democracy and a capitalistic society. People learn these things from

- parents
- teachers
- friends
- coworkers
- church
- clubs
- sports
- mass media

CLASS NOTES

Political socialization differs for people.

- children identify with a country
- college students form their opinions based on their experiences
- older people try to influence public policies that will affect their lives
- people with more education and income take more of an active part in politics
- people similar in age go through the same political experiences.

CLASS NOTES

_____

_____

_____

_____

_____

_____

_____

_____

_____

_____

_____

_____

_____

_____

_____

_____

_____

_____

_____

_____

_____

CHAPTER 7

Public Opinion

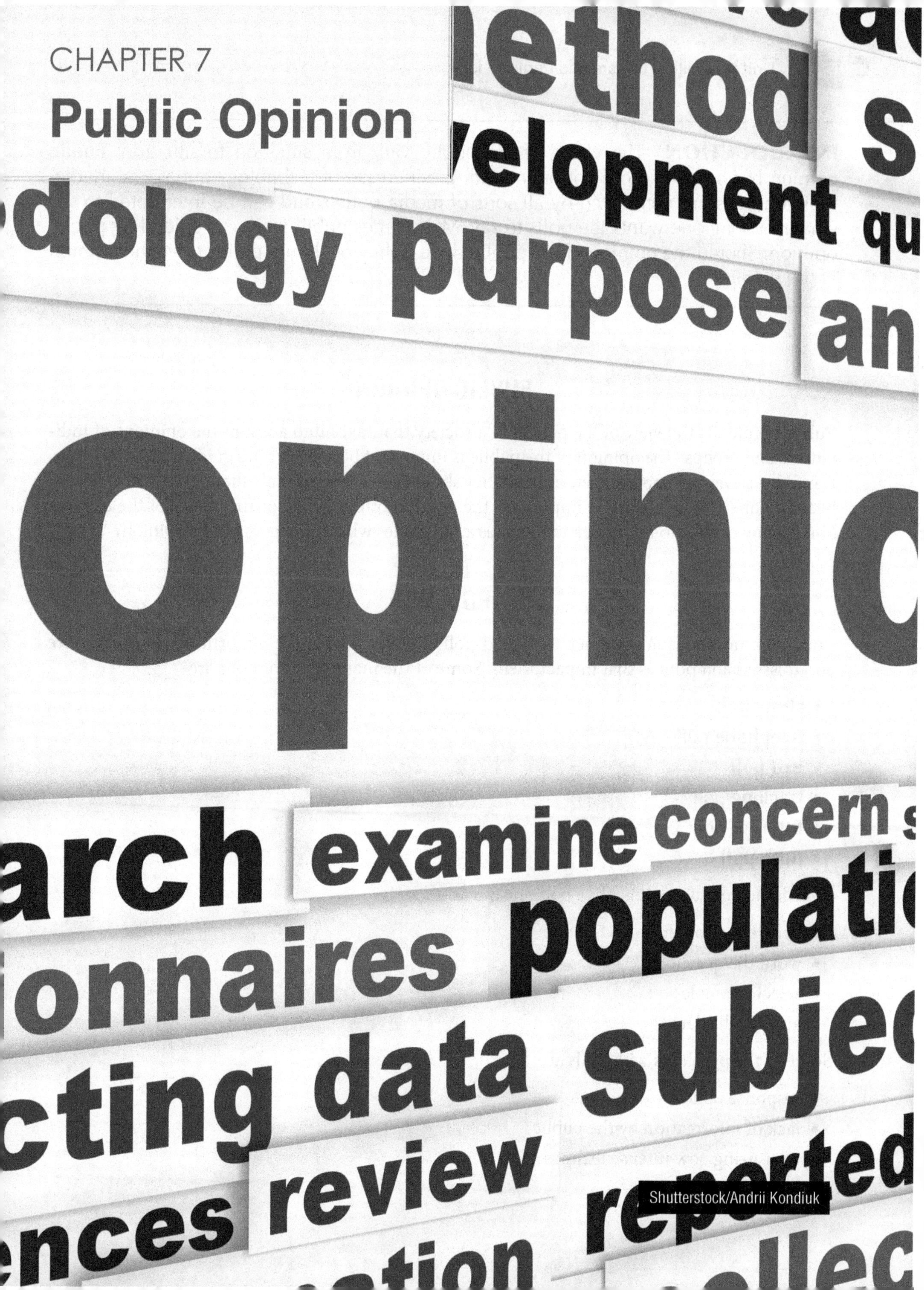

Shutterstock/Andrii Kondiuk

INTRODUCTION The views of the public vary from situation to situation. **Public opinion** has become more important with the increase of technology and social media. Opinion polls are conducted by all sorts of media outlets and can be interpreted to say whatever someone wants the polls to say. Many times public policy is guided by public opinion. Should the opinion of the public drive policy or should policy drive the opinion of the public?

PUBLIC OPINION

Public opinion is the view of the people in a society that takes into account the opinions of individuals and groups. The opinion of the public is important because it does guide policy decisions. Candidates even take polls to determine if they should run for a political office or not. The question becomes one of which is more important, the opinion of the public or the advice of the experts. Since many people do not understand issues and policies what influences public opinion?

POLLING

Public opinion polls are not new. Detailed polling gives people the opportunity to learn more about issues and polices that impact them. Some of the many types of polls are

- straw poll
- telephone poll
- exit poll
- tracking poll
- Internet poll
- push poll

In order to conduct an effective poll one must

- decide the content
- word the questions
- select a sample
- analyze the data

Some of the problems with polls are

- response options
- lack of information by the public
- measuring how intense feelings are
- lack of interest

CLASS NOTES

CHAPTER 8

Types of Elections and Voting

INTRODUCTION   In the United States, we have multiple elections on the federal, state, and local levels. All of these elections give voters the opportunity to choose the people who make decisions that we all have to live by. Elections are vital to show that the power is given by the people, or consent of the governed. **Incumbents** have an advantage in elections. Participation in election process by voting is important but being an informed voter is more important because it can only make the process better. Are you a voter or an informed voter?

TYPES OF ELECTIONS

There are many types of elections in which the **electorate** participate. Most of these elections are for the purpose of picking candidates to fill public offices. Other elections allow the electorate to make public policy or remove officials from office.

> **Primary elections**—elections to pick a candidate from a party for the general election
>> **Open primary**—primary where anyone can participate
>> **Closed primary**—primary limited to members of a particular party
>> **Crossover voting**—voting in a primary of the other party
>> **Runoff primary**—primary between the top two candidates from the first primary
>
> **General elections**—election to pick the candidate that will fill a particular office
> **Initiative**—election allowing voters to propose legislation
> **Referendum**—election where state legislatures propose legislation voter approval
> **Recall**—election to remove someone from office before the next election
> **Presidential elections**—election every 4 years to pick the President
>> **Electoral College**—the process to pick the President
>
> **Congressional elections**—every 2 years to pick members of the House and Senate
> **Mid-term elections**—elections held between presidential elections

PARTICIPATION AND VOTING

Political participation takes on many forms.

- voting
- volunteering in political activities
- joining political parties
- contacting officials
- working in campaigns

CLASS NOTES

_____

_____

_____

_____

_____

_____

_____

_____

_____

_____

_____

_____

_____

_____

_____

_____

_____

_____

_____

_____

- monetary contributions
- run for public office
- protesting

INFLUENCES ON VOTING AND VOTER TURNOUT

There are many things that influence how people vote and whether or not they even vote. Some of those are

- political parties
- ideology
- income and education
- race and ethnicity
- gender
- religion
- issues
- interest in politics

Some reasons given by people for not voting are

- too busy
- illness or emergency
- not interested
- don't like candidates
- out of town
- don't know
- registration problems
- inconvenient polling place
- forgot
- transportation problems
- bad weather

VOTING REFORMS

In order to get more people to vote, there have been numerous reforms suggested. Some of them are

- make election day a national holiday
- early voting
- mail and online voting
- easier registration
- standardize the process

CLASS NOTES

ELECTION

CAMPAIGN

INTRODUCTION   In order for a candidate to win an election, they must run an effective **campaign**. The campaign must influence people to vote for the candidate in the nomination, primary, and general elections. An effective campaign takes a great staff, lots of money, and the ability to reach potential voters. Above all, an effective campaign has a message of ideas to share with potential voters.

THE CANDIDATE

A candidate runs for a particular office for many reasons. They may have a specific objective, personal ambition, or feel they can do a better job than the person that currently holds that office. The candidate must be someone that is likable, trustworthy, and one that the voters believe in. They, and their families, must be able to withstand the scrutiny of the media and their opponent.

CAMPAIGN STAFF

A campaign staff plans strategy, writes speeches, conducts polls, and decides how to get the candidate's message out to potential voters. A good campaign staff includes the following:

Campaign Manager
Finance Chair
Communications Staff
    Communications Director
    Press Secretary
Campaign Consultants
    Pollsters
Volunteers

RAISING MONEY

In order for a candidate to win an election, it takes lots of money to get their message out to the voters. The money comes from many sources and there have been efforts to regulate the ways campaigns raise and spend money.

Regulations
    Federal Elections Campaign Act (FECA)
    Bipartisan Campaign Reform Act (BCRA)
        Hard money
        Soft money

CLASS NOTES

Sources
    Individuals
    Political parties
    Political Action Committees (PACs)
    Member PACs
    Personal savings
    Public funds
        Matching funds
    Soft money groups
        527 Political Committees
        501(c) Groups

GETTING THE MESSAGE OUT

The media is the main way a candidate gets their message out to potential voters. They do this through the traditional media, the new media, and campaign advertisements.

    Traditional media
        Reporters
        Staged events
        Spin
        Talk shows
        Debates
    New media
        Phone messages or Robo calls
        Internet
            Web sites
            Blogs
    Campaign advertisements
        Positive Ads
        Negative Ads
        Contrasting Ads

CLASS NOTES

CHAPTER 10
Political Parties

INTRODUCTION A **political party** is an organized group of people with similar political goals who want to gain power and influence public policy by winning elections. Although there are many political parties, the United States is considered a two-party system. Those two parties are the Democratic and Republican Parties. The two parties differ in their philosophy about the role the government should play in the lives of the citizens. There are third, or minor, parties that are many times issue based. These issues are many times ones neglected by the two major parties. Our political system makes it hard for these third parties to win major elections.

FUNCTIONS OF POLITICAL PARTIES

Run candidates for office

- raise money
- gain support
- get people to vote

Formulate and promote policy

national party platform

Organize the government
Create unity and accountability

PARTY IDENTIFICATION

How people and groups identify with a particular political party depends on many factors such as

geographic region
gender
race and ethnicity
age
religion
marital status
social and economic status

CLASS NOTES

INTRODUCTION **Interest groups** are people or organizations that try to influence public policy. Many times we call them special interests, lobbying groups, public interest groups, or pressure groups. They all try to influence the decisions of the government on the issues most important to them. These groups are successful because of the leadership they have, funding, and membership.

KINDS OF INTEREST GROUPS

Public interest groups

- seek a collective good

Economic interest groups

- promote the economic interest of members

Government interest groups

- state and local governments
- **earmarks**

Political Action Committees (PACs)

- fundraising organizations that represent interest groups

ACTIVITIES OF INTEREST GROUPS

Lobbying

- Congress
- Executive Branch
- Courts
- People

Elections

- Recruit and endorse candidates
- Encourage people to vote
- Rate candidates or people in office
- Make campaign contributions

CLASS NOTES

REGULATIONS ON INTEREST GROUPS

Federal Regulation of Lobbying Act

- required registration of lobbyists

Lobbying Disclosure Act

- stricter definition of lobbying
- tougher registration requirements
- reporting of clients and issues
- estimate amount paid by clients

Honest Leadership and Open Government Act

- longer waiting periods before becoming a lobbyist and bans on gifts

CLASS NOTES

CHAPTER 12
Legislative Branch

Shutterstock/J Main

INTRODUCTION The **Legislative Branch** is the lawmaking body of the government. This branch is called Congress. It is made up of the House of Representatives and the Senate. The members of the House and Senate are voted into office by the voters in the state or district in which they live. The Framers believed that this branch was very important and put it first in the Constitution. The role of representatives and senators today has become more than just that of a lawmaker. They must also deal with the budget, make policy, and still represent their state or district. Every Congress has a 2-year term and each term is numbered.

THE HOUSE OF REPRESENTATIVES

What the Constitution says

- 25 years of age
- 7 years a U.S. citizen
- resident of the district
- membership apportioned by population (currently 435 members)
- 2-year term
- initiates all revenue bills
- initiates **impeachment** procedures and articles of impeachment

Operation

- Committee on Rules is powerful
- stresses tax and revenue policy

Leadership

- Speaker of the House
- Majority leader
- Majority whip
- Minority leader
- Minority whip

THE SENATE

What the Constitution says

- 30 years of age
- 9 years a U.S. citizen
- resident of the state

CLASS NOTES

_____

_____

_____

_____

_____

_____

_____

_____

_____

_____

_____

_____

_____

_____

_____

_____

_____

_____

_____

_____

_____

- membership consists of two per state (100 members)
- 6-year term (1/3 of Senate up for reelection every 2 years)
- gives "advice and consent" on presidential appointments
- approves treaties
- tries impeached officials

Operation

- **filibuster** and **cloture**
- stresses foreign policy

Leadership

- President of the Senate (Vice President of the United States)
- President pro tempore
- Majority leader
- Majority whip
- Minority leader
- Minority whip

CONSTITUTIONAL POWERS OF CONGRESS

- lay and collect taxes and duties
- borrow money on the credit of the United States
- regulate commerce with foreign nations and the states
- establish rules for **naturalization** (immigration or the process of becoming a citizen)
- establish rules for bankruptcy
- coin money, regulate its value, and fix the standard of weights and measures
- punish counterfeiting
- establish post offices and post roads
- issues patents and copyrights
- define and punish piracies and felonies committed on the high seas
- create courts inferior to the Supreme Court
- declare war
- raise and support an army and a navy and make rules for governing them
- provide for a militia
- exercise legislation over the District of Columbia and federal facilities
- make all laws necessary and proper to carry out the above powers
  - **Necessary and Proper Clause**

CLASS NOTES

BEING THE INCUMBENT

- the **incumbent** is the person currently in office
- advantages
  - people know who you are
  - you can show constituents what you have done for them
  - you have a staff in place to help constituents and run a campaign
  - you and your staff have worked with the media
  - fund raising is easier since there is a high reelection rate

CLASS NOTES

CHAPTER 13
Executive Branch

INTRODUCTION   The **Executive Branch** is made up of the presidency and the governmental bureaucracy. This is the branch of government charged with enforcing the laws. A President's term is defined many times by circumstances beyond their control. The method of electing the President is through the **Electoral College**. In this process, the people do not directly vote for the President. They vote for electors that directly vote for the President and Vice President. The President is considered the figurehead of the government and the most powerful leader in the world.

THE PRESIDENT

What the Constitution says

- natural-born citizen
- 35 years of age
- resident of the United States for at least 14 years
- 4-year terms
    - two terms

Powers in the Constitution

- appoint Cabinet, federal judges, and ambassadors
- convene Congress
- make treaties
- **veto** (no line-item veto)
- Commander-in-Chief
- pardon power

Presidential roles

- **Chief Executive**
- **Chief Diplomat**
- **Commander-in-Chief**
- **Legislative leader**
- **Head of State**
- **Economic leader**
- **Party leader**

Presidential succession

- Vice President
- Speaker of the House

CLASS NOTES

- President Pro Tempore of the Senate
- Secretary of State
- Secretary of the Treasury
- Secretary of Defense
- Attorney General
- Secretary of the Interior
- Secretary of Agriculture
- Secretary of Commerce
- Secretary of Labor
- Secretary of Health and Human Services
- Secretary of Housing and Urban Development
- Secretary of Secretary of Transportation
- Secretary of Energy
- Secretary of Education
- Secretary of Veterans Affairs
- Secretary of Homeland Security

THE BUREAUCRACY

The bureaucracy consists of the thousands of government agencies that **implement** federal laws, programs, and regulations through their **discretion**. Many times it is called the "fourth branch of government." **Bureaucrats** are career government employees that work in Cabinet level departments and independent agencies that implement the laws, programs, and regulations. Cabinet secretaries are nominated by the President and confirmed by the Senate. They remain in office for the duration of that president.

Organization

- Cabinet departments (advise the President relating to duties for their offices)
  - **State** (foreign affairs and relations with other nations)
  - **Treasury** (economic, financial, tax, and fiscal policies)
  - **Defense** (military forces needed to deter and protect country)
  - **Justice** (enforces and defends federal laws)
  - **Interior** (national conservation efforts)
  - **Agriculture** (cares for food, agriculture, range lands, and forest)
  - **Commerce** (promotes economic, business, and job opportunities)
  - **Labor** (protects workers' wages, health, and safety)
  - **Health and Human Services** (protects health and provides human services)
  - **Housing and Urban Development** (decent home living environment)

CLASS NOTES

- ○ **Transportation** (efficient, accessible, safe, and convenient transportation)
- ○ **Energy** (develop reliable energy systems)
- ○ **Education** (guidelines for education system)
- ○ **Veterans Affairs** (advocate for veterans and their families)
- ○ **Homeland Security** (prevent terrorist attacks within the United States)
- Independent executive agencies
- Independent regulatory commissions
- Government corporations

Political Involvement

- Hatch Act
- Federal Employees Political Activities Act of 1993

Concerns

- Borrowing of money
- Retirement programs

CLASS NOTES

CHAPTER 14
Judicial Branch

EQUAL JUSTICE UNDER LAW

INTRODUCTION   The **Judicial Branch** of government interprets the laws. The Constitution created the U.S. Supreme Court and inferior courts created by Congress, defined the
jurisdiction of the Supreme Court, and defined treason. The Judiciary Act of 1789 created
a federal court system consisting of the U.S. Supreme Court, U.S. Courts of Appeals, and
U.S. District Courts. **Judicial review** was established by the Marbury v Madison decision.
The federal system handles both **criminal law** and **civil law**. Federal judges are appointed
for a life term.

*came about the Marbury v. Madison case
not in the Constitution*

FEDERAL COURTS

U.S. Supreme Court
- **Original jurisdiction**
  - two or more states
  - the United States and a state
  - foreign ambassador and other diplomats
  - a state and a citizen of another state
- **Appellate jurisdiction**
  - from U.S. courts of appeals
  - state Supreme Court
  - Court of Military Appeals
- ***Writ of Certiorari***
- **Rule of Four**
- **Briefs**
- ***Amicus Curiae* Briefs**
- Decisions
  - **majority opinion**
  - **concurring opinion**
  - **dissenting opinion**
- **Judicial Restraint**
- **Judicial Activism**
- ***Stare Decisis***

CLASS NOTES

_____

_____

_____

_____

_____

_____

_____

_____

_____

_____

_____

_____

_____

_____

_____

_____

_____

_____

_____

_____

U.S. Courts of Appeals

- Original jurisdiction
  - none
- Appellate jurisdiction
  - lower federal courts
  - U.S. regulatory commissions
  - legislative courts

U.S. District Courts

- Original jurisdiction
  - federal government as a party
  - civil suits under federal law
  - civil suits between citizens of different states ($75,000.00)
  - Admiralty or maritime disputes
  - bankruptcy
  - other matters assigned by Congress
- Appellate jurisdiction
  - none

CLASS NOTES

Domestic and Economic Policy

INTRODUCTION   The government's role in handling issues within the country varies. **Domestic policies** are the laws, programs, and decisions dealing with issues within the country. These are designed to protect citizens from poverty, improve their health, help them maintain a healthy environment, and live productive lives. **Economic policies** are the things the government does to handle and influence the economy. These things encourage economic development and make tax and income security policies.

THE STEPS OF THE POLICY-MAKING PROCESS

1. Recognition of a problem
2. Setting of an agenda
3. Formulating a policy
4. Adopting a policy
5. Setting a budget for the policy
6. Implement the policy
7. Evaluate the policy

DOMESTIC POLICIES

Health care

Medicare (provides medical care for the elderly usually 65 and up)
- Usually covers 80% of costs
- Part A (covers hospitalization)
- Part B (optional and covers doctor's visits and outpatient services)
- Part C (Medicare Advantage that covers gaps in coverage)
- Part D (optional drug benefit)

Medicaid (helps to provide medical care for the poor)
- Must meet income eligibility requirements
- A national and state government program
  - federal block grants usually cover 50–75%

Health insurance (national, personal, or through employer)
- Costs are rising
  - technology advances
  - longer lifespan

CLASS NOTES

_____

_____

_____

_____

_____

_____

_____

_____

_____

_____

_____

_____

_____

_____

_____

_____

_____

Public health
- Protecting public health
  - immunizations
  - education
  - advertisements
  - regulations

Medical research

Obesity

Education

Accountability
- Standardized tests, report cards, reorganization, and teacher evaluations

Flexibility
- Schools are free from some regulations to spend money to meet their needs

Best practices
- Proven methods to achieve quality outcomes

School choice
- **Vouchers**
- Charter schools

Energy

Oil and other fossil fuels

Natural gas

Solar

Wind

Consumption

Environmental

National Environmental Policy Act of 1969

Clean Air Act of 1970

Clean Water Act of 1972

Safe Drinking Water Act of 1974

National Energy Policy Plan of 1981

Clean Air Act of 1990

Energy Policy Act of 1992

Climate Change

CLASS NOTES

ECONOMIC POLICIES

Social regulations
Economic regulations
Deregulation
Fiscal Policy
The **Budget**

- Raising money
- Spending money
- **Deficit**
- **Debt**
- **Inflation**

Monetary Policy

- **The Federal Reserve (The Fed)**

Income Security

- **Entitlement programs**
- **Nonmeans-tested programs**
- **Means-tested programs**
- **Social Security**
- **Unemployment Insurance**
- Supplemental Security Income
- Family and Child Support
- Earned Income Tax Credit
- Supplemental Nutrition Assistance Program

CLASS NOTES

CHAPTER 16
Foreign and Defense Policy

INTRODUCTION   How the government deals with other countries and issues throughout the world is the process of **diplomacy**. It encompasses foreign and defense policy. **Foreign policy** is the process of how a country creates and maintains a relationship with another country in order to protect its own national interest. **Defense policy** is the strategy a country uses to protect itself from its enemies. These policies have changed over the years because of technology and terrorism that have made isolationism a thing of the past.

WORLD WAR II

International Monetary Fund
World Bank

COLD WAR

Truman Doctrine
Marshall Plan
North Atlantic Treaty Organization (NATO)
Bay of Pigs
Cuban Missile Crisis
Vietnam and the **Domino Theory**
Richard Nixon and **detente**

- SALT I
- SALT II
- **War Powers Act**

Jimmy Carter and human rights
Reagan Doctrine

AFTER THE COLD WAR AND TERRORISM

George H.W. Bush and the Persian Gulf War
Bill Clinton and the concept of **enlargement**
George W. Bush and 9–11

- War in Afghanistan
- War in Iraq

Counterterrorism Policy

CLASS NOTES

NUCLEAR WEAPONS

Disarmament
North Korea
Iran

TRADE

North American Free Trade Agreement (NAFTA)
World Trade Organization (WTO)

IMMIGRATION

Border security
Legal v illegal
Amnesty

WHO IS INVOLVED

Executive Branch

- President
- Department of State
- Department of Defense
- Department of Homeland Security
- Intelligence Community

Legislative Branch

- Congress
  - Oversight
  - Treaties
  - Executive Agreements
  - Appointments
  - Appropriations
  - War Powers Act

CLASS NOTES

Glossary

Chapter 1

Constitution   a document that establishes the framework of government

Ratified   passed or approved

Founding Fathers   those who made significant contributions to the Constitution

Framers   those who wrote the Constitution

Compromise   a way to reach an agreement in which each side gives up something to get something

Preamble   the statement at the beginning of the Constitution stating the source of its authority and purpose

Popular Sovereignty   political authority rests with the people

Federalism   a system of government dividing the power between a national and state and local governments

Limited Government   the government may only do what the people, or Constitution, direct it to do

Separation of Powers   the division of governmental power among the three equal branches

Checks and Balances   where each branch of government limits the power of the other two branches

Judicial Review   the power of the courts to determine if the actions of the other branches are constitutional

Necessary and Proper Clause   gives Congress the authority to pass laws to carry out the enumerated powers

Electoral College   the body of electors chosen in each state to elect the President and the Vice President

State of the Union Address   an annual message to Congress in which the President proposes his legislative program

Full Faith and Credit Clause   where states will honor the laws and judicial proceedings of other states

Bill of Rights   the first 10 amendments to the Constitution that list the rights of the people

Suffrage   the right to vote

Poll Taxes   a tax that had to be paid before someone could voteFull Faith and Credit

Chapter 2

Nullification   the right of a state to declare a federal law void

Dual Federalism   separate and equally powerful levels of government are best

Cooperative Federalism   federal and state governments work together to solve problems

Competitive Federalism   responsibilities are assigned based on who is best to handle the task

Enumerated Powers   specific powers granted to Congress in the Constitution

Naturalization   the legal process by which a person becomes a citizen

Reserved Powers   powers the 10th Amendment gives the states

Concurrent Powers   powers shared by the national and state governments

Devolution   returning powers to the states

Unfunded Mandates   national laws directing states to comply with regulations with no funding

Chapter 3

Civil Liberties   the personal guarantees and freedoms that the government cannot take away

Establishment Clause   where the government cannot establish or sanction an official religion

Free Exercise Clause   where the government will not interfere with the practice of religion

Prior Restraint   prohibiting speech or publication before the fact

Symbolic Speech   symbols, signs, and other methods of expression

Hate Speech   speech attacking a person/group because of gender, ethnic origin, religion, disability, or sexual orientation

Libel   written word that is false and damages a person's character

Slander   spoken word that is false and damages a person's character

Fighting Words   words that cause injury or incite a breach of the peace

Exclusionary Rule   rule that anything seized illegally cannot be used in court

Miranda Warning   the right to remain silent and the right to an attorney if needed

Double Jeopardy   can't be tried twice for the same crime

Eminent Domain   the right of the government to take private property for public use

Due Process   legal requirement that all legal rights owed to a person must be respected

Chapter 4

Civil Rights   the rights of individuals against discriminatory treatment based on race, sex, national origin, age, religion, or sexual orientation

Plessy v Ferguson   established separate but equal as the law of the land

Brown v Board of Education of Topeka Kansas   overturned Plessy v Ferguson in education and became the law of the land

Jim Crow   laws that separated the races in the south

Affirmative Action   policies used to give special treatment to all groups that have been discriminated against

Regents of the University of California v Bakke   reverse discrimination case stating that strict affirmative action quotas were inappropriate

Grutter v Bollinger   upheld the affirmative action policies that gave preference to minority students

Chapter 5

News   reports by journalists of selected events

Mass Media   the established methods of communication designed to reach large audiences

New Media   electronic communications through the use of digital technology

Social Media   communities created online where ideas and information are shared

Narrowcasting   when the media targets its programming to specific groups in society

Objectivity   reporting the news impartially without opinion

"On the Record"   information released and attributed by name to the source

"Off the Record"   information that will not be released to the public

Press Release   document offering an official position

Press Briefing   restricted session between an aide and the press

Press Conference   unrestricted session between an official and the press

Sound Bites   comments spoken by individuals that are brief and compelling

Talking Heads   person giving information on TV where only the head or shoulders are shown

Pundits   a person who knows a lot about a subject and speaks out about it

Partisans   strong supporter of a party, cause, or person

Experts   person with a high degree of skill or knowledge in a specific area

Spin   interpret something in a way to sway public opinion

Watchdog   when the media stories hold people in power accountable

Attack dog   when media stories are very negative and focus on blunders and scandals

Chapter 6

Melting pot   a society where many different types of people blend together as one

Political Culture   shared beliefs, values, and attitudes on how government should operate

American Exceptionalism   belief that America is unique based on our founding and principles

Political Socialization   how individuals get their political beliefs and values

Chapter 7

Public Opinion   what the public thinks about an issue at any point in time

Straw Poll   unscientific survey used to gauge public opinion on issues

Telephone Poll   survey conducted through landline phones or cell phones

Exit Poll   poll taken as voters leave their voting location

Tracking Poll   survey that charts a candidate's daily rise or fall in support

Internet Poll   survey conducted online

Push Poll   survey taken that provides information to lead people to vote against someone

Chapter 8

Incumbents   the person currently in office

Electorate   citizens eligible to vote

Primary Elections   election to decide a candidate to represent a party in the general election

Open Primary   primary in which all of the electorate can vote

Closed Primary   primary in which only registered party members can vote

Crossover Voting   voting in the primary of the other party

Runoff Primary   a second primary election between the top two candidates from the primary

General Elections   election in which the voters pick the candidate to fill a specific office

Initiative   election that allows citizens to propose legislation or constitutional amendments

Referendum   election where the state legislature proposes legislation or amendments

Recall   election where voters can remove an incumbent from office

Presidential Elections   elections held every 4 years to pick a candidate to be the President

Electoral College   representatives from each state who cast ballots that elect the President

Congressional Elections   elections held every 2 years to elect members to Congress

Mid-term Elections   elections held in the middle of a presidential term

Chapter 9

Political Action Committees (PACs)   officially registered fund-raising organization

Public Funds   money from general tax revenues to campaigns

Matching Funds   donations to presidential campaigns matching money raised by the candidate

527 Political Committees   tax-exempt group created to raise money for political activities

501(c) Groups   nonprofit, tax-exempt group not subject to FEC disclosure rules

Spin   putting out the most favorable interpretation for a candidate

Positive Ads   advertising that good points of a candidate with no reference to the opponent

Negative Ads   advertising for a candidate that attacks the opponent's character or platform

Contrasting Ads   advertising that compares the records and platforms of candidates

Chapter 10

Political Party   group of individuals who organize to win elections and operate the government

National Party Platform   a statement of the general and specific goals of a political party

Chapter 11

Interest Groups   collection of people or organizations that try to influence public policy

Public Interest Groups   a group that seeks a collective that may or may benefit them

Economic Interest Groups   a group that promotes the economic interests of their members

Earmarks   funds in an appropriations bill for specific projects

Political Action Committees (PACs)   officially registered fund-raising organization

Lobbying   trying to influence legislation that will benefit their organization

Chapter 12

Legislative Branch   the lawmaking body of the government

Impeachment   formal process of accusing an official of unlawful activity

Filibuster   when the minority party in the Senate blocks a vote by unlimited debate

Cloture   the 60 vote minimum required to stop debate and end a filibuster

Naturalization   the formal process in which a noncitizen can become a citizen

Necessary and Proper Clause   gives Congress the power to carry out the enumerated powers

Incumbent   the person currently holding an office

Chapter 13

Executive Branch   the branch of government that enforces laws

Electoral College   the process of electing the President

Chief Executive   manages the government

Chief Diplomat   directs foreign policy

Commander-in-Chief   in charge of the military and makes military decisions

Legislative leader   suggests laws and uses influence to get laws passed

Head of State   symbolic and ceremonial leader of the United States

Economic leader   monitors the economy and plans the federal budget

Party Leader   supports fellow party members and raises campaign funds

Veto   formal process of rejecting bills passed by Congress

Implement   putting a law or policy into operation

Discretion   freedom to decide what should be done

Bureaucrats   career government employees that implement laws, programs, and regulations

Department of State   handles foreign affairs and relations with other nations

Department of Treasury   handles economic, financial, tax, and fiscal policies

Department of Defense   handles military forces needed to deter and protect the country

Department of Justice   enforces and defends federal laws

Department of Interior   handles national conservation efforts

Department of Agriculture   cares for food, agriculture, rand lands, and forest

Department of Commerce   promotes economic, business, and job opportunities

Department of Labor   protects workers' wages, health, and safety

Department of Health and Human Services   protects health and provides human services

Department of Housing and Urban Development   decent home living environment

Department of Transportation   efficient, accessible, safe, and convenient transportation

Department of Energy   develop reliable energy systems

Department of Education   guidelines for education system

Department of Veterans Affairs   advocate for veterans and their families

Department of Homeland Security   prevent terrorist attacks within United States

Chapter 14

Judicial Branch   the branch of government that interprets the laws

Judicial Review   reviewing actions and laws to determine if they are constitutional

Criminal Law   laws related to protection of property and individual safety

Civil Law   laws related to relationships between individuals and groups

Original Jurisdiction   jurisdiction of courts that hear cases for the first time

Appellate Jurisdiction   courts that review findings of law by lower courts

Writ of Certiorari   request of the Supreme Court to review records of a lower court

Rule of Four   when at least four Supreme Court justices vote to hear a case

Briefs   legal written arguments in a case

Amicus Curiae Briefs   "Friend of the court" briefs based on interests

Majority Opinion   the decision of a Supreme Court case

Concurring Opinion   agreeing the majority decision, but for a different reason

Dissenting Opinion   disagreeing with the majority decision

Judicial Restraint   the view that the decisions of other branches should stand

Judicial Activism   judges should use their power to further justice

Stare Decisis   reliance on previous decisions to decide new cases

Chapter 15

Domestic Policies   laws, programs, and decisions dealing with issues within the country

Economic Policies   things the government does to handle and influence the economy

Medicare   the federal program that provides medical care for the elderly usually 65 and up

Medicaid   a government program that helps to provide medical care for the poor

Vouchers   certificates issued by the government to help pay the cost of private or public school

Climate Change   increase in global temperatures due to carbon emissions from fossil fuels

Social Regulations   government regulation of consumer protection, health, and safety

Economic Regulations   government regulation of business practices

Deregulation   a reduction in market controls in favor of market-based competition

Fiscal Policy   government's taxing and spending policies to maintain economic stability

Budget   an itemized estimate of expenses and the income to finance them

Deficit   spending more money than is received

Debt   the amount of money borrowed and must be paid back

Inflation   rise in the price levels of the economy

Monetary Policy   regulation where the money supply and interest rates are regulated

The Federal Reserve (The Fed)   the central banking system of the United States

Income Security   programs that protect people from a loss of income for a variety of reasons

Entitlement Programs   benefits where people meeting the requirements legally receive

Nonmeans-Tested Programs   programs that provide cash assistance regardless of income

Means-Tested Programs   programs that provide cash assistance based on income

Social Security   provides old age insurance as well as for others that qualify

Unemployment Insurance   insurance for full-time employees who become unemployed

Chapter 16

Diplomacy   the art of negotiating with other nations

Foreign Policy   building relationships with other countries to protect national interests

Defense Policy   the strategy a country uses to protect itself from its enemies

International Monetary Fund   created to stabilize international currency transactions

World Bank   create to provide loans for large economic development projects

Truman Doctrine   to provide economic and military assistance to fight communism

Marshall Plan   provide American aid to Western Europe after WWII

North Atlantic Treaty Organization (NATO)   security pact between the United States and Europe

Domino Theory   if one country falls to communism the others near it would fall as well

Detente   improvement in U.S.–Soviet relations during the 1970s

War Powers Act   limits the President's ability to send troops into conflict indefinitely

Reagan Doctrine   provide military assistance to anti-communist groups

Enlargement   promote the expansion of democracy and free markets throughout the world

North American Free Trade Agreement (NAFTA)   free movement of goods and services between the United States, Canada, and Mexico

World Trade Organization (WTO)   created to supervise and open international trade

CPSIA information can be obtained at www.ICGtesting.com
Printed in the USA
LVOW02s0835140615

442406LV00002B/2/P